# The Iraqi
## HOME COOK

## GARDEN of GRAPES.

First Edition: 2024

Published by Garden of Grapes.

Printed in USA

The recipes, techniques, and tips in this cookbook are intended for personal use only. The author and publisher are not responsible for any adverse effects or consequences resulting from the use of the recipes or suggestions in this book.

Library of Congress Cataloging-in-Publication Data:

First edition.
Includes index.

Manufactured in USA

# Introduction

Welcome, culinary adventurers and lovers of Middle Eastern cuisine, to "The Iraqi Home Cook: Experience Iraqi Gastronomy - A Middle Eastern Cookbook with 100+ Recipes and Stunning Pictures." Within these pages, you are about to embark on a delightful culinary journey through the rich and diverse flavors of Iraq.

This cookbook is a celebration of the rich culinary heritage, aromatic spices, and cherished culinary traditions of Iraq, inviting you to explore the unique blend of Middle Eastern, Persian, and Levantine influences that define Iraqi cuisine. Each recipe is a reflection of the country's rich cultural tapestry and its deep-rooted traditions of hospitality and culinary excellence.

My inspiration for creating this cookbook stems from a deep love and appreciation for the culinary treasures of Iraq, as well as a desire to share its rich gastronomic heritage with the world. Having had the privilege of experiencing the warmth and hospitality of Iraqi home cooks firsthand, I wanted to create a collection of recipes that would capture the essence of their kitchens and allow readers to savor the flavors of this captivating country in their own homes.

So, dear readers, prepare to tantalize your taste buds and embark on a culinary adventure through the flavors of Iraq with "The Iraqi Home Cook." Whether you're a seasoned chef or a novice in the kitchen, this cookbook promises to delight your senses, inspire your culinary creativity, and transport you to the heart of the Middle East. Bon appétit, and may your culinary journey be filled with joy, flavor, and discovery!

# Cooking Philosophy or Approach

In the mosaic of Middle Eastern cuisine, where flavors intertwine and traditions flourish, "The Iraqi Home Cook" invites you to embark on a culinary voyage through the rich tapestry of Iraqi gastronomy. With over 100 recipes that embody the essence of this ancient land, this cookbook serves as a portal to the diverse and flavorful world of Iraqi cuisine, inviting you to experience the vibrant flavors and rich heritage of this storied land.

Our approach to cooking and food is rooted in a deep reverence for the culinary traditions of Iraq and a commitment to preserving the authenticity of its flavors. We celebrate the rich array of ingredients that grace Iraqi tables, from the earthy flavors of lamb and rice to the aromatic spices that perfume the air. Each recipe is a celebration of the culinary artistry that defines Iraqi cuisine, from the comforting warmth of biryani to the tantalizing flavors of dolma.

But what truly sets "The Iraqi Home Cook" apart is its emphasis on home cooking and the intimate connection between food and family. Each recipe is a labor of love, passed down through generations and perfected over time. From hearty stews and comforting soups to fragrant rice dishes and indulgent desserts, every dish tells a story of tradition, hospitality, and the joy of sharing a meal with loved ones.

So gather your ingredients, fire up your stove, and let "The Iraqi Home Cook" be your guide to discovering the flavors of Iraq. Here's to savoring the rich heritage and vibrant flavors of this ancient land, one delicious recipe at a time.

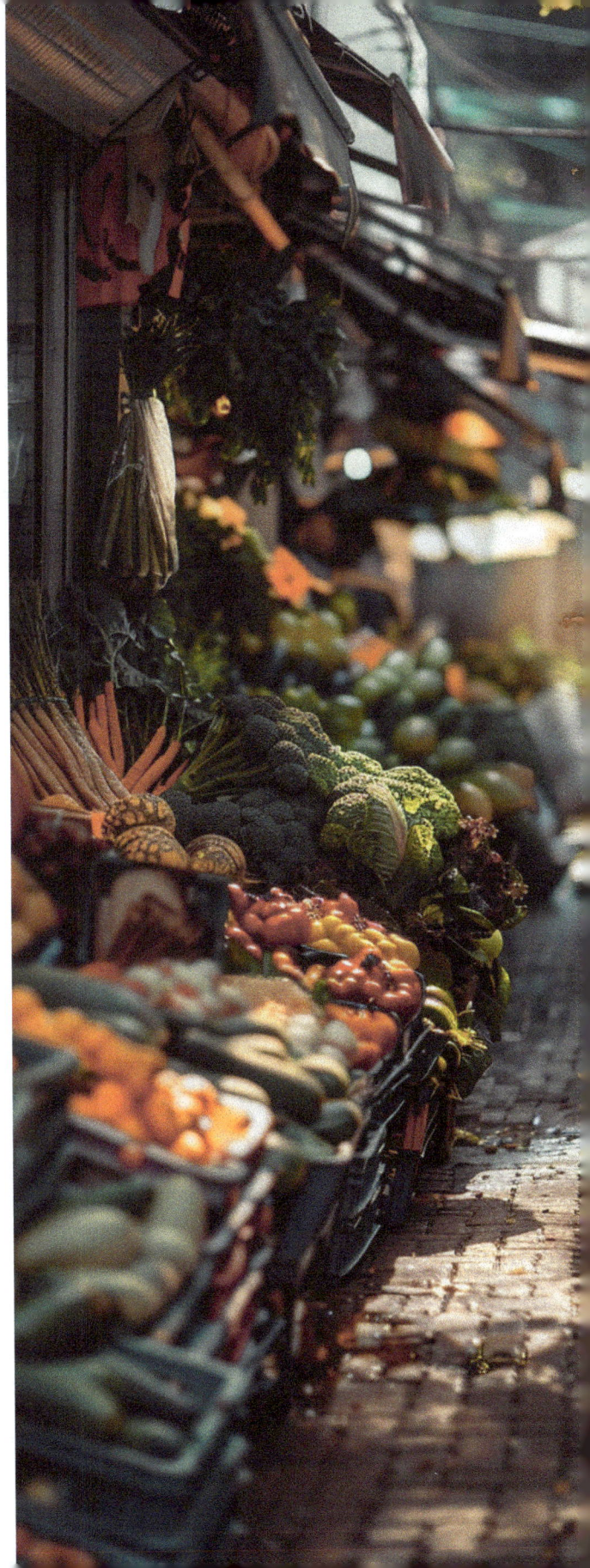

# Tips for Successful Cooking

Welcome to The Iraqi Home Cook, an exhilarating voyage through the savory and aromatic delights of Iraq. Within the pages of this culinary masterpiece, you'll uncover a treasure trove of recipes that unveil the essence and spirit of Iraqi gastronomy. But before we embark on this epicurean expedition, let's fortify our culinary prowess with some indispensable guidance for successful cooking.

First and foremost, let's delve into the fundamentals. Every proficient cook understands the pivotal role of preparation. Prior to igniting the flames, take a moment to peruse the recipe in its entirety. Familiarize yourself with the ingredients, tools, and techniques required. This preliminary step serves as a beacon, steering you clear of potential culinary pitfalls.

Now, let's explore the realm of ingredient selection. In Iraqi cuisine, the mantra is freshness reigns supreme. Whenever feasible, opt for locally sourced, seasonal ingredients. Not only will they exude peak flavor and nutritional potency, but they also champion the cause of local farmers and artisans. Embrace the adventurous spirit of Iraqi cooking by fearlessly experimenting with an array of herbs, spices, and seasonings. After all, the heart of Iraqi cuisine pulsates with bold and tantalizing flavors.

Next on our culinary agenda is the art of preparation. Whether you're dicing vegetables, marinating meats, or toasting spices, precision is paramount. Dedicate ample time to ensuring uniformity in your chopping, thoroughness in your marination, and accuracy in your spice measurements. This meticulous attention to detail during the preparatory phase serves as the bedrock upon which culinary triumphs are erected.

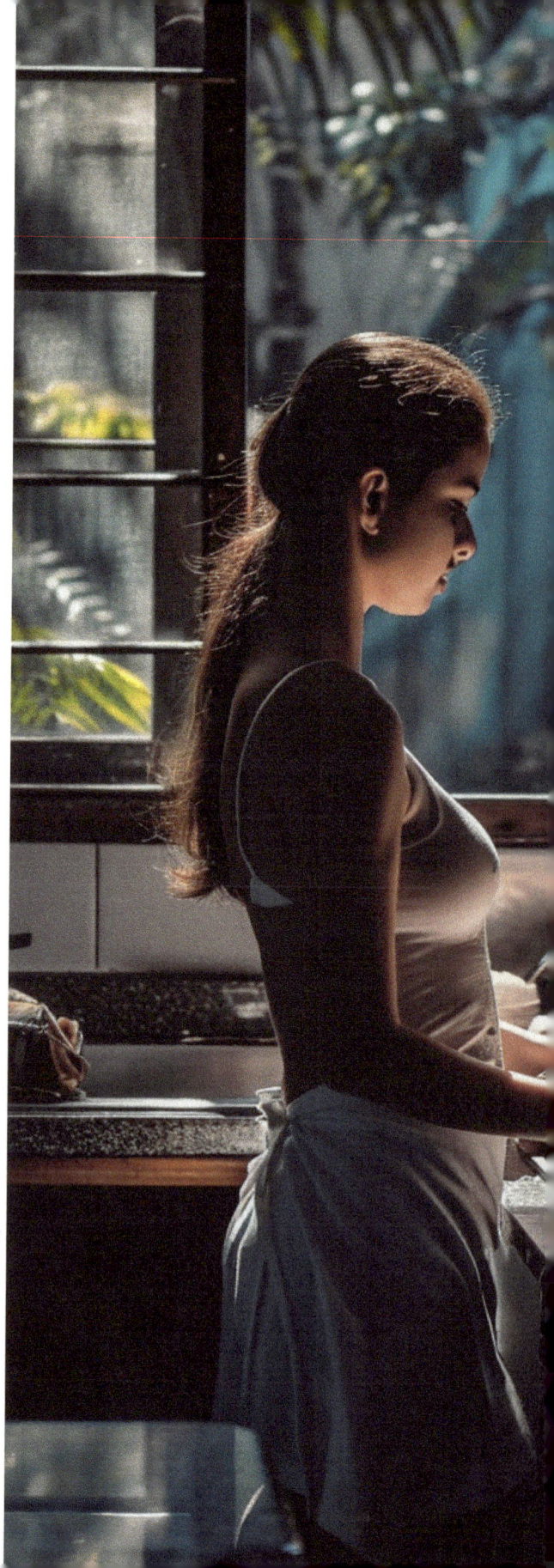

Let's now navigate through the labyrinth of cooking methods. Iraqi gastronomy boasts a rich tapestry of culinary techniques, ranging from slow braising to swift sautéing, from charcoal grilling to oven baking. Each method bestows its own distinctive nuances of flavor and texture upon the dish. Embrace the opportunity to acquaint yourself with these diverse techniques, for in the realm of cooking, versatility is the hallmark of mastery.

Lastly, let's celebrate the art of presentation. In Iraqi culture, meals are not merely sustenance—they are veritable feasts for the senses. Elevate your culinary creations by adorning them with care, embellishing with fresh herbs or a drizzle of fragrant olive oil, and serving them with pride. Remember, a meticulously presented dish not only tantalizes the eyes but also gratifies the palate.

Armed with these indispensable insights, you are now equipped to embark on your culinary voyage through The Iraqi Home Cook. With a spirit of adventure and a dash of creativity, prepare to immerse yourself in the rich and diverse tapestry of Iraqi gastronomy. So don your aprons, sharpen your knives, and let the culinary odyssey commence!

# Kitchen Essentials

Welcome to the rich tapestry of Iraqi gastronomy, where ancient traditions and vibrant flavors come together to create a culinary experience like no other. Join us as we journey through the diverse and delicious dishes of Iraq with "Experience Iraqi Gastronomy," a Middle Eastern cookbook featuring over 100 recipes that celebrate the unique flavors and ingredients of this captivating country.

Kitchen Essentials:

### 1. Mangal (Grill):
Embrace the tradition of outdoor cooking with a mangal, essential for grilling meats, kebabs, and vegetables to perfection. Whether powered by charcoal or gas, a mangal allows you to infuse your dishes with the irresistible smoky flavor that is characteristic of Iraqi cuisine.

### 2. Tandoor Oven:
Experience the art of baking bread in a traditional tandoor oven, perfect for preparing Iraqi flatbreads such as khubz and samoon. The intense heat of the tandoor oven results in breads that are crisp on the outside and tender on the inside, with a deliciously charred flavor that pairs perfectly with savory stews and dips.

### 3. Mortar and Pestle:
Unlock the bold flavors of Iraqi spices and herbs with a mortar and pestle, essential for grinding and blending aromatic ingredients. Whether preparing baharat spice blends, harissa pastes, or za'atar seasoning, a mortar and pestle allows you to create custom spice mixes that elevate your dishes to new heights.

### 4. Iraqi Tea Set:
Experience the warmth and hospitality of Iraqi culture with a traditional Iraqi tea set, complete with a teapot, glasses, and a decorative tray. Brew fragrant Iraqi tea infused with cardamom and served with a side of sugar cubes, a symbol of friendship and hospitality in Iraqi households.

# Kitchen Essentials

Tips for Effective Use:

## 1. Mangal Mastery:
Preheat your mangal before adding ingredients to ensure even cooking and beautiful grill marks. Use high-quality charcoal or hardwood for the best flavor, and adjust the height of the grill grate as needed to control the cooking temperature.

## 2. Tandoor Oven Techniques:
Shape bread dough into rounds or ovals and slap them onto the inner walls of the tandoor oven, where they will adhere and bake to perfection. Rotate the breads regularly with a long-handled tool to ensure even cooking, and brush them with ghee or butter immediately after removing them from the oven for added flavor.

## 3. Mortar and Pestle Expertise:
Grind spices and herbs in small batches using a mortar and pestle to ensure maximum flavor and aroma. Experiment with different combinations of spices to create your own signature blends, and store them in airtight containers to preserve their freshness.

## 4. Iraqi Tea Ritual:
Brew Iraqi tea slowly over low heat, allowing the flavors of the cardamom to infuse into the water. Serve the tea in small glasses alongside sugar cubes or rock candy, and take the time to savor each sip while enjoying the company of friends and family.

## 5. Kubba Mold Wisdom:
Use a kubba mold to shape and fill the kubba mixture, ensuring that each dumpling is uniform in size and shape. Press the filled kubba firmly to seal the edges and prevent the filling from leaking out during cooking, and fry them until golden and crisp on the outside.

With these essential tools and expert tips at your disposal, you're well-equipped to experience Iraqi gastronomy and savor the flavors of the Middle East in every dish.

# Flavor Pairing Suggestions

Welcome to "The Iraqi Home Cook," a culinary voyage where we invite you to experience the rich and diverse flavors of Iraqi gastronomy through a Middle Eastern cookbook featuring over 100 authentic recipes accompanied by stunning pictures. In this culinary exploration, we celebrate the vibrant culinary heritage and warm hospitality of Iraq.

Before we delve into the delightful recipes that await, let's take a moment to appreciate the cultural richness and culinary traditions that inspire each dish. Iraqi cuisine is a reflection of the country's history, geography, and diverse cultural influences, blending flavors from the Middle East, Persia, and the Levant. From aromatic rice dishes and hearty stews to succulent grilled meats and delectable desserts, each recipe offers a taste of the diverse and vibrant culinary landscape of Iraq.

So, dear reader, prepare to indulge your senses and embark on a journey through the flavors and aromas of Iraq. With "The Iraqi Home Cook" as your guide, let's explore the delicious flavors and rich culinary heritage of this enchanting Middle Eastern country, one mouthwatering recipe at a time.

# Table of content

# Chapter 1:
# Starters and Appetizers

1 serving

15 minutes

# Hummus with Olive Oil Drizzle

Easy

## Ingredients:

1 can (15 oz) chickpeas
3 tbsp tahini
2 tbsp lemon juice
2 cloves garlic, minced
Salt to taste
3 tbsp olive oil
Paprika for garnish
Fresh parsley, chopped

Hummus with Olive Oil Drizzle is a classic Middle Eastern dip that has gained worldwide popularity. Its origins trace back to ancient Egypt, where it was enjoyed for its creamy texture and flavorful blend of chickpeas, tahini, and spices.

## Directions

1. Drain and rinse chickpeas.
2. In a food processor, blend chickpeas, tahini, lemon juice, garlic, and salt until smooth.
3. Transfer to a serving bowl and drizzle with olive oil.
4. Sprinkle with paprika and chopped parsley.
5. Serve with pita bread or vegetables.

## Insider Tips

Use canned white beans as a substitute for chickpeas.

1 serving

40 minutes

# Baba Ganoush

## Ingredients:

2 medium eggplants
3 tbsp tahini
2 tbsp lemon juice
2 cloves garlic, minced
Salt to taste
2 tbsp olive oil
Parsley for garnish

Baba Ganoush is a smoky eggplant dip originating from the Middle East. Its popularity stems from its unique flavor profile, combining roasted eggplant, tahini, garlic, and lemon juice.

## Directions

1. Preheat oven to 400°F (200°C). Roast eggplants until tender, about 30 minutes.
2. Scoop out the flesh and mash it.
3. Mix mashed eggplant with tahini, lemon juice, garlic, and salt.
4. Drizzle with olive oil and garnish with parsley.
5. Serve with pita bread or vegetables.

## Insider Tips

Use yogurt as a substitute for tahini.

**1 serving**

**20 minutes**

**Easy**

# Fattoush Salad

## Ingredients:

1 cup lettuce, chopped
1 cucumber, diced
1 tomato, diced
1/4 cup red onion, thinly sliced
1/4 cup radishes, sliced
1/4 cup fresh mint leaves, chopped
1/4 cup fresh parsley, chopped
1/4 cup toasted pita bread, torn
2 tbsp olive oil
2 tbsp lemon juice
Salt and pepper to taste

Fattoush Salad is a refreshing Lebanese salad that combines crisp vegetables, herbs, and toasted bread. Its origins date back centuries and it remains a beloved dish for its vibrant flavors.

## Directions

1. In a large bowl, combine chopped lettuce, cucumber, tomato, onion, radishes, mint, and parsley.
2. Add toasted pita bread pieces.
3. Drizzle with olive oil, lemon juice, salt, and pepper.
4. Toss gently to combine.
5. Serve immediately.

## Insider Tips

Use any available seasonal vegetables.

# Tabbouleh

## Ingredients:

1/2 cup bulgur wheat
1 cup parsley, chopped
1/4 cup mint leaves, chopped
2 tomatoes, diced
1 cucumber, diced
1/4 cup red onion, finely chopped
2 tbsp olive oil
2 tbsp lemon juice
Salt and pepper to taste

1 serving

25 minutes

Easy

Tabbouleh is a refreshing Lebanese salad made with bulgur wheat, fresh herbs, and vegetables. Its origins date back to ancient times and it's known for its vibrant colors and zesty flavors.

## Directions

1. Rinse bulgur wheat and soak in hot water until tender, about 15 minutes.
2. Drain excess water from bulgur.
3. In a bowl, combine bulgur with chopped parsley, mint, tomatoes, cucumber, and onion.
4. Drizzle with olive oil, lemon juice, salt, and pepper.
5. Toss to combine.
6. Chill before serving.

## Insider Tips

Use quinoa instead of bulgur for a gluten-free option.

**1 serving**

**60 minutes**

**Normal**

# Stuffed Grape Leaves (Dolma)

## Ingredients:

1/2 cup rice, cooked
1/4 cup fresh dill, chopped
1/4 cup fresh mint, chopped
1/4 cup parsley, chopped
1/4 cup pine nuts
1/4 cup currants or raisins
1/2 tsp cinnamon
Salt and pepper to taste
15-20 grape leaves, rinsed and drained
2 tbsp olive oil
2 cups vegetable broth

## Insider Tips

Use quinoa instead of rice for a healthier option.

Stuffed Grape Leaves, also known as Dolma, are a Mediterranean delicacy filled with seasoned rice and herbs. They have a long history, dating back to ancient times, and are enjoyed for their savory taste.

## Directions

1. In a bowl, mix cooked rice with dill, mint, parsley, pine nuts, currants, cinnamon, salt, and pepper.
2. Place a grape leaf flat on a surface and add a spoonful of the rice mixture.
3. Roll the leaf, tucking in the sides to form a neat package.
4. Repeat with remaining leaves and filling.
5. Place stuffed grape leaves in a pot, seam side down.
6. Pour vegetable broth and olive oil over the grape leaves.
7. Cover and simmer for 45 minutes to 1 hour.
8. Serve warm or chilled.

**Normal**

1 serving

45 minutes

# Kibbeh (Baked or Fried)

## Ingredients:

1 cup bulgur
1 lb ground lamb or beef
1 onion, finely chopped
2 tsp ground cumin
2 tsp ground coriander
Salt and pepper to taste
Vegetable oil for frying (if frying)

Kibbeh, a Middle Eastern delight, features a savory blend of ground meat, bulgur, onions, and spices, either baked or fried to golden perfection.

## Directions

1. Soak bulgur in hot water for 15-20 minutes until softened; drain excess water.
2. In a bowl, mix bulgur, ground meat, chopped onion, cumin, coriander, salt, and pepper.
3. Form mixture into small balls or patties.
4. To bake: Preheat oven to 375°F, place kibbeh on a baking sheet, and bake for 20-25 minutes until cooked through.
5. To fry: Heat vegetable oil in a skillet, fry kibbeh until golden brown on all sides, about 5-7 minutes per side.
6. Serve hot with tahini sauce or yogurt sauce.

## Insider Tips

Use ground chicken or turkey instead of lamb or beef.
Substitute quinoa for bulgur if desired.
Bake kibbeh in an air fryer for a healthier option.

**1 serving**

**120 minutes**

# Iraqi Samoon Bread

## Ingredients:

4 cups all-purpose flour
2 tsp active dry yeast
1 1/2 cups warm water
1 tsp salt
2 tbsp olive oil
Sesame seeds for topping (optional)

## Insider Tips

Use whole wheat flour for a healthier option.
Add herbs like thyme or oregano for extra flavor.
Brush bread with melted butter after baking for
a richer taste.

**Normal**

Iraqi Samoon Bread is a soft and chewy flatbread, perfect for dipping into savory stews or enjoying with grilled meats.

## Directions

1. In a bowl, dissolve yeast in warm water and let it sit for 5 minutes until frothy.
2. Add flour, salt, and olive oil; knead until a smooth dough forms.
3. Cover and let it rise in a warm place for 1 hour until doubled in size.
4. Preheat oven to 400°F.
5. Divide dough into balls and flatten into rounds.
6. Place on a baking sheet, brush with water, and sprinkle with sesame seeds.
7. Bake for 15-20 minutes until golden brown.
8. Serve warm with butter or as a side to your favorite dishes.

**1 serving**   **10 minutes**

# Labneh with Za'atar

## Ingredients:

2 cups plain yogurt
1/2 tsp salt
1 tbsp olive oil
1 tbsp za'atar spice blend

Easy

Labneh with Za'atar is a creamy and tangy yogurt cheese spread, drizzled with olive oil and sprinkled with za'atar spice blend.

## Directions

1. In a bowl, mix yogurt and salt.
2. Place a cheesecloth or muslin over a bowl, pour yogurt mixture, and tie the cloth.
3. Hang the cloth to drain excess liquid for 8-12 hours in the fridge.
4. Transfer labneh to a serving dish, drizzle with olive oil, and sprinkle with za'atar.
5. Serve with pita bread or as a dip for veggies.

## Insider Tips

Use Greek yogurt for a thicker consistency.
Add minced garlic for extra flavor.
Substitute za'atar with dried herbs and sesame seeds.

**4 servings**

**20 minutes**

# Falafel

## Ingredients:

1 cup dried chickpeas
1/2 large onion
2 cloves garlic
1/4 cup fresh parsley
1 tsp cumin
1 tsp coriander
1/4 tsp cayenne pepper
Salt and pepper to taste
1 tsp baking powder
4 tbsp flour
Vegetable oil for frying

**Easy**

Originating from the Middle East, falafel has become a beloved street food worldwide. These crispy chickpea fritters are packed with flavor and perfect for a quick and satisfying meal.

## Directions

1. Soak chickpeas in water overnight. Drain and pat dry.
2. In a food processor, combine chickpeas, onion, garlic, parsley, cumin, coriander, cayenne, salt, pepper, baking powder, and flour. Pulse until mixture is coarse but well blended.
3. Shape mixture into small patties.
4. Heat oil in a skillet over medium heat. Fry falafel until golden brown and crispy.
5. Serve hot with tahini sauce and pita bread.

## Insider Tips

If chickpeas are unavailable, you can use canned chickpeas (drained and rinsed) as a substitute. For a gluten-free version, use chickpea flour instead of regular flour.

**6 servings**  **40 minutes**

**Easy**

# Lentil Soup

## Ingredients:

1 cup dried lentils
1/2 onion
2 carrots
2 stalks celery
2 cloves garlic
1 bay leaf
1 tsp cumin
1/2 tsp paprika
Salt and pepper to taste
6 cups vegetable broth
Fresh parsley for garnish

Lentil soup has been a staple in many cultures for centuries. This hearty and nutritious dish is perfect for chilly days, offering a comforting blend of flavors and textures.

## Directions

1. Rinse lentils under cold water.
2. In a large pot, sauté onion, carrots, celery, and garlic until softened.
3. Add lentils, bay leaf, cumin, paprika, salt, pepper, and vegetable broth.
4. Bring to a boil, then reduce heat and simmer for 30 minutes or until lentils are tender.
5. Remove bay leaf and blend soup until smooth.
6. Serve hot with a sprinkle of fresh parsley.

## Insider Tips

Substitute vegetable broth with chicken broth for a non-vegetarian version.
Add diced tomatoes or spinach for extra flavor and nutrients.

12 pieces

45 minutes

Normal

# Spinach Fatayer

## Ingredients:

2 cups all-purpose flour
1 tsp yeast
1/2 tsp sugar
1/2 cup warm water
1/4 cup olive oil
1/2 tsp salt
2 cups fresh spinach
1/2 onion
2 tbsp lemon juice
1/2 tsp sumac
Salt and pepper to taste

## Insider Tips

Use frozen spinach if fresh is unavailable. Substitute sumac with lemon zest for a similar tangy flavor.

Originating from the Middle East, spinach fatayer are savory pastries filled with a delicious spinach and onion mixture. These handheld treats are perfect for snacks or light meals.

## Directions

1. In a bowl, mix flour, yeast, sugar, water, oil, and salt. Knead until dough is smooth. Cover and let rise for 1 hour.
2. Meanwhile, sauté spinach, onion, lemon juice, sumac, salt, and pepper until spinach wilts. Let cool.
3. Divide dough into 12 balls. Roll each ball into a circle.
4. Place spinach mixture in the center of each circle. Fold edges to form a triangle.
5. Bake at 350°F (175°C) for 20-25 minutes or until golden brown.
6. Serve warm or at room temperature.

# Chapter 2:
# Soups and Stews

1 serving

30 minutes

Easy

# Iraqi Red Lentil Soup

## Ingredients:

1/2 cup red lentils
2 cups water
1 small onion (chopped)
1 medium carrot (chopped)
1 celery stalk (chopped)
2 garlic cloves (minced)
1 teaspoon ground cumin
1/2 teaspoon ground coriander
Salt and pepper to taste
Fresh lemon juice for garnish
Chopped fresh cilantro or parsley for garnish

Originating from the heart of Iraqi kitchens, Shorbat Adas is a soul-warming soup that has stood the test of time. Its popularity lies in its simplicity and robust flavors, making it a staple in Iraqi households.

## Directions

1. Rinse the lentils and combine them with water in a pot. Bring to a boil, then reduce heat and simmer for 15 minutes.
2. Add onion, carrot, celery, garlic, cumin, coriander, salt, and pepper. Cook until vegetables are tender, about 10 minutes.
3. Blend the soup until smooth. Adjust seasoning if needed.
4. Serve hot with a squeeze of lemon juice and a sprinkle of fresh herbs.

## Insider Tips

Use green lentils if red lentils are unavailable.

# Lamb and Okra Stew

**1 serving**  **90 minutes**

## Ingredients:

1/2 lb lamb stew meat
1 cup fresh or frozen okra
1 onion (chopped)
2 garlic cloves (minced)
1 can diced tomatoes
1 tablespoon tomato paste
1 teaspoon ground coriander
1 teaspoon ground cumin
Salt and pepper to taste
Fresh cilantro or parsley for garnish
Cooked rice or bread for serving

**Normal**

Bamia, the beloved Lamb and Okra Stew of Iraq, embodies a harmonious blend of tender lamb, vibrant okra, and aromatic spices. Its popularity stems from its hearty nature, making it a comforting dish for gatherings and special occasions.

## Directions

1. Brown the lamb in a pot over medium heat. Add onion and garlic, cook until softened.
2. Stir in tomatoes, tomato paste, coriander, cumin, salt, and pepper. Add water to cover the meat.
3. Simmer for 1 hour, then add okra and cook until tender.
4. Adjust seasoning and serve hot with rice or bread, garnished with fresh herbs.

## Insider Tips

Substitute beef for lamb if preferred. Use frozen okra if fresh is not available.

1 serving

45 minutes

# Chicken and Rice Soup

## Ingredients:

1/2 lb chicken breast (cubed)
1/2 cup rice
1 onion (chopped)
2 carrots (sliced)
2 celery stalks (chopped)
2 garlic cloves (minced)
1 teaspoon ground turmeric
1/2 teaspoon ground cumin
Salt and pepper to taste
Fresh parsley or dill for garnish
Lemon wedges for serving

## Insider Tips

Use bone-in chicken for added flavor.

Easy

Shorbat Dajaj, a comforting Chicken and Rice Soup from Iraq, is a nourishing bowl of goodness that soothes the soul. Its popularity lies in its simplicity and wholesome flavors, making it a go-to dish for cold days or when feeling under the weather.

## Directions

1. In a pot, sauté onion, carrots, celery, and garlic until softened. Add chicken and cook until browned.
2. Stir in rice, turmeric, cumin, salt, and pepper. Add water and simmer until rice and chicken are cooked.
3. Adjust seasoning and serve hot with a sprinkle of fresh herbs and a squeeze of lemon.

**1 serving**

**40 minutes**

# Eggplant and Tomato Stew

## Ingredients:

1 large eggplant (cubed)
2 tomatoes (chopped)
1 onion (chopped)
2 garlic cloves (minced)
1 teaspoon ground cumin
1/2 teaspoon paprika
Salt and pepper to taste
Fresh parsley for garnish
Cooked rice or bread for serving

**Easy**

This Eggplant and Tomato Stew is a delightful fusion of flavors from Iraq, showcasing the versatility of eggplants in Middle Eastern cuisine. Its popularity is owed to the harmonious blend of tomatoes, spices, and tender eggplant, creating a dish that is both comforting and full of character.

## Directions

1. Sauté onion and garlic until translucent. Add eggplant and cook until softened.
2. Stir in tomatoes, cumin, paprika, salt, and pepper. Cook until tomatoes are tender.
3. Adjust seasoning and serve hot with rice or bread, garnished with fresh parsley.

## Insider Tips

Use canned tomatoes if fresh ones are not available.

🍽️ 1 serving ⏰ 60 minutes

# Iraqi White Bean Soup

## Ingredients:

1 cup dried white beans (soaked overnight)
1 onion (chopped)
2 carrots (chopped)
2 celery stalks (chopped)
2 garlic cloves (minced)
1 teaspoon ground cumin
1/2 teaspoon ground coriander
Salt and pepper to taste
Fresh cilantro or parsley for garnish
Lemon wedges for serving

**Normal**

Shorbat Lubia, the comforting Iraqi White Bean Soup, is a hearty bowl of goodness that warms the soul. Its popularity lies in its simplicity and nourishing qualities, making it a staple in Iraqi cuisine.

## Directions

1. Drain soaked beans and add to a pot with onion, carrots, celery, garlic, cumin, coriander, salt, and pepper. Add water to cover.
2. Simmer until beans are tender, about 45 minutes to 1 hour.
3. Adjust seasoning and serve hot with fresh herbs and lemon wedges.

## Insider Tips

Use canned white beans if soaking overnight is not possible.

Iraqi White Bean Soup (Shorbat Lubia),18

Easy

# Tashreeb (Iraqi Bread Soup)

## Ingredients:

2 cups stale bread, torn into pieces
1 onion, chopped
2 cloves garlic, minced
2 tomatoes, diced
1/2 cup cooked chickpeas
1/2 tsp turmeric
1/2 tsp cumin
1/2 tsp paprika
Salt and pepper to taste
4 cups vegetable broth
2 tbsp olive oil

Tashreeb is a comforting Iraqi dish that transforms leftover bread into a hearty soup. Its origins date back to ancient times, where resourcefulness in the kitchen led to the creation of this flavorful and satisfying meal.

## Directions

1. In a pot, sauté onion and garlic in olive oil until translucent.
2. Add tomatoes, chickpeas, turmeric, cumin, paprika, salt, and pepper.
3. Cook for 5 minutes.
4. Pour in vegetable broth and bring to a boil.
5. Reduce heat and simmer for 10 minutes.
6. Add torn bread pieces and simmer until bread is soft.
7. Adjust seasoning as needed.
8. Serve hot with a drizzle of olive oil.

## Insider Tips

Use any type of bread, such as pita or French bread.

**Easy**

# Chickpea and Spinach Stew

## Ingredients:

- 1 can (15 oz) chickpeas, drained and rinsed
- 2 cups fresh spinach
- 1 onion, chopped
- 2 cloves garlic, minced
- 1 can (14 oz) diced tomatoes
- 1 tsp ground cumin
- 1 tsp ground coriander
- 1/2 tsp paprika
- Salt and pepper to taste
- Olive oil for cooking
- Fresh cilantro for garnish
- Cooked rice or bread for serving

Delight in the wholesome flavors of Chickpea and Spinach Stew, a nourishing blend of tender chickpeas, vibrant spinach, and aromatic spices simmered to perfection, offering a comforting and nutritious meal for any occasion.

## Directions

1. In a pot, heat olive oil over medium heat.
2. Sauté chopped onion and minced garlic until translucent.
3. Add chickpeas, diced tomatoes, ground cumin, ground coriander, paprika, salt, and pepper.
4. Simmer for 15 minutes until flavors meld.
5. Stir in fresh spinach until wilted.
6. Adjust seasoning as needed.
7. Garnish with fresh cilantro.
8. Serve hot with cooked rice or bread.

## Insider Tips

- Use canned spinach if fresh spinach is unavailable.

**1 serving**

**60 minutes**

Normal

# Beef and Potato Stew

## Ingredients:

- 1 lb beef stew meat, cubed
- 2 potatoes, peeled and diced
- 1 onion, chopped
- 2 carrots, sliced
- 2 cloves garlic, minced
- 1 can (14 oz) beef broth
- 1 cup water
- 1 tbsp tomato paste
- 1 tsp dried thyme
- 1 tsp dried rosemary
- Salt and pepper to taste
- Olive oil for cooking
- Fresh parsley for garnish
- Crusty bread for serving

## Insider Tips

- Use chicken or lamb stew meat for variation.

Indulge in the hearty flavors of Beef and Potato Stew, a comforting dish filled with tender beef, wholesome potatoes, and aromatic herbs and spices, creating a satisfying meal that warms the soul.

## Directions

1. In a Dutch oven or large pot, heat olive oil over medium-high heat.
2. Add cubed beef and brown on all sides.
3. Remove beef and set aside.
4. Sauté chopped onion and minced garlic until fragrant.
5. Add diced potatoes, sliced carrots, beef broth, water, tomato paste, dried thyme, dried rosemary, salt, and pepper.
6. Bring to a boil, then reduce heat and simmer for 40 minutes until beef and vegetables are tender.
7. Adjust seasoning as needed.
8. Garnish with fresh parsley.
9. Serve hot with crusty bread.

1 serving

45 minutes

Easy

# Lentil and Vegetable Soup

## Ingredients:

- 1 cup dried lentils, rinsed
- 2 carrots, diced
- 2 celery stalks, diced
- 1 onion, chopped
- 2 cloves garlic, minced
- 1 can (14 oz) diced tomatoes
- 4 cups vegetable broth
- 1 tsp ground cumin
- 1 tsp ground turmeric
- 1/2 tsp ground coriander
- Salt and pepper to taste
- Olive oil for cooking
- Fresh parsley for garnish
- Lemon wedges for serving

## Insider Tips

- Use chicken broth instead of vegetable broth.

Experience the comforting goodness of Lentil and Vegetable Soup, a hearty blend of nutritious lentils, colorful vegetables, and aromatic spices, creating a wholesome and flavorful dish that's perfect for chilly days.

## Directions

1. In a pot, heat olive oil over medium heat.
2. Sauté chopped onion and minced garlic until fragrant.
3. Add diced carrots, diced celery, and rinsed lentils.
4. Stir in diced tomatoes, vegetable broth, ground cumin, ground turmeric, ground coriander, salt, and pepper.
5. Bring to a boil, then reduce heat and simmer for 30 minutes until lentils are tender.
6. Adjust seasoning as needed.
7. Garnish with fresh parsley.
8. Serve hot with a squeeze of lemon.

# Chicken Harira Soup

Normal

1 serving

45 minutes

~~~~~~~~~~~~~~~~~

## Ingredients:

- 1 lb boneless chicken thighs, cubed
- 1 can (15 oz) chickpeas, drained and rinsed
- 1 onion, chopped
- 2 carrots, diced
- 2 celery stalks, diced
- 2 cloves garlic, minced
- 1 can (14 oz) diced tomatoes
- 6 cups chicken broth
- 1/4 cup chopped fresh cilantro
- 1/4 cup chopped fresh parsley
- 1 tsp ground cumin
- 1 tsp ground turmeric
- 1/2 tsp ground cinnamon
- Salt and pepper to taste
- Olive oil for cooking
- Lemon wedges for serving
- Cooked rice or bread for serving

## Insider Tips

- Use canned chickpeas instead of dried for convenience.

Delve into the rich flavors of Chicken Harira Soup, a Moroccan-inspired dish featuring tender chicken, hearty chickpeas, and a medley of spices and herbs, offering a comforting and soul-warming bowl of goodness.

## Directions

1. In a Dutch oven or large pot, heat olive oil over medium heat.
2. Sauté chopped onion and minced garlic until fragrant.
3. Add cubed chicken and brown on all sides.
4. Stir in diced carrots, diced celery, drained chickpeas, diced tomatoes with their juices, chicken broth, ground cumin, ground turmeric, ground cinnamon, salt, and pepper.
5. Bring to a boil, then reduce heat and simmer for 30 minutes until chicken and vegetables are cooked through.
6. Stir in chopped fresh cilantro and parsley.
7. Adjust seasoning as needed.
8. Serve hot with a squeeze of lemon and cooked rice or bread.

# Chapter 3:
# Main Dishes - Meat

**1 serving**

**120 minutes**

Normal

# Iraqi Lamb Kebabs

## Ingredients:

- 1 lb lamb (cut into cubes)
- 1 onion (grated)
- 2 cloves garlic (minced)
- 2 tbsp yogurt
- 1 tbsp olive oil
- 1 tsp paprika
- 1 tsp cumin
- Salt and pepper to taste
- Skewers (soaked in water)
- Fresh herbs (for garnish)

These succulent Iraqi Lamb Kebabs are a flavorful delight, blending tender lamb with aromatic spices, perfect for any occasion.

## Directions

1. In a bowl, mix grated onion, minced garlic, yogurt, olive oil, paprika, cumin, salt, and pepper.
2. Marinate lamb cubes in this mixture for at least 1 hour.
3. Thread lamb onto skewers and grill until cooked through.
4. Garnish with fresh herbs before serving.

## Insider Tips

Use beef or chicken instead of lamb.

1 serving    90 minutes

# Iraqi Chicken Tikka

## Ingredients:

- 1 lb chicken (cut into cubes)
- 1/2 cup yogurt
- 2 tbsp lemon juice
- 2 cloves garlic (minced)
- 1 tsp ginger (grated)
- 1 tsp cumin
- 1 tsp coriander
- 1/2 tsp turmeric
- Salt and pepper to taste
- Skewers (soaked in water)
- Fresh cilantro (for garnish)

Iraqi Chicken Tikka is a crowd-pleaser, featuring tender chicken marinated in a blend of spices, grilled to perfection.

## Directions

1. Combine yogurt, lemon juice, minced garlic, grated ginger, cumin, coriander, turmeric, salt, and pepper in a bowl.
2. Marinate chicken cubes in this mixture for at least 30 minutes.
3. Thread chicken onto skewers and grill until fully cooked.
4. Garnish with fresh cilantro before serving.

## Insider Tips

Use boneless lamb or beef instead of chicken.

Easy

1 serving

30 minutes

# Iraqi Style Grilled Fish

## Ingredients:

- 1 lb fish fillets (such as tilapia or cod)
- 2 tbsp olive oil
- 1 tbsp lemon juice
- 1 tsp paprika
- 1/2 tsp cumin
- Salt and pepper to taste
- Fresh parsley (chopped, for garnish)

Enjoy the flavors of Iraq with this delicious Iraqi Style Grilled Fish, seasoned with spices and grilled to perfection.

## Directions

1. Preheat grill and brush fish fillets with olive oil.
2. Season with lemon juice, paprika, cumin, salt, and pepper.
3. Grill fish for 5-7 minutes per side until cooked through.
4. Garnish with chopped parsley before serving.

## Insider Tips

Use any firm-fleshed fish of your choice.

1 serving

180 minutes

# Lamb Mansaf

## Ingredients:

- 1 lb lamb (cut into pieces)
- 2 cups yogurt
- 1 onion (chopped)
- 2 cloves garlic (minced)
- 1/2 cup almonds (toasted)
- 1/2 cup pine nuts (toasted)
- 1 tsp turmeric
- Salt and pepper to taste
- Cooked rice
- Fresh parsley (chopped, for garnish)

Lamb Mansaf is a traditional Iraqi dish, featuring tender lamb cooked in yogurt sauce, served over fragrant rice.

## Directions

1. Brown lamb pieces in a pan, then add chopped onion and minced garlic.
2. Pour yogurt over lamb, add turmeric, salt, and pepper. Simmer until lamb is tender.
3. Toast almonds and pine nuts in a separate pan.
4. Serve lamb over cooked rice, garnished with nuts and parsley.

## Insider Tips

Use chicken instead of lamb for a variation.

1 serving

90 minutes

# Iraqi Biryani

## Ingredients:

- 1 lb chicken or lamb (cut into pieces)
- 2 cups basmati rice
- 1 onion (sliced)
- 2 tomatoes (chopped)
- 1/2 cup yogurt
- 2 tbsp ghee or butter
- 1 tsp cumin
- 1 tsp coriander
- 1/2 tsp cinnamon
- Salt and pepper to taste
- Fresh cilantro (chopped, for garnish)

Normal

Iraqi Biryani is a fragrant and flavorful rice dish, layered with tender meat and aromatic spices, a true culinary delight.

## Directions

1. Cook rice until almost done, then drain and set aside.
2. In a pan, sauté onion in ghee until golden.
3. Add meat, tomatoes, yogurt, cumin, coriander, cinnamon, salt, and pepper. Cook until meat is tender.
4. Layer rice and meat mixture in a pot, cover, and simmer until flavors blend.
5. Garnish with chopped cilantro before serving.

## Insider Tips

Use beef instead of lamb or chicken for a different taste.

# Chicken Shawarma

## Ingredients:

- 200g chicken breast, thinly sliced
- 1/4 cup yogurt
- 2 tbsp olive oil
- 1 tbsp lemon juice
- 1 tsp paprika
- 1 tsp cumin
- 1/2 tsp turmeric
- 2 cloves garlic, minced
- Salt and pepper to taste
- Pita bread
- Lettuce, tomatoes, onions, cucumbers (for serving)
- Tahini sauce or garlic sauce (for serving)

Chicken Shawarma, a Middle Eastern delight, features marinated and grilled chicken wrapped in pita bread with fresh veggies and a tangy sauce.

## Directions

1. In a bowl, mix yogurt, olive oil, lemon juice, paprika, cumin, turmeric, garlic, salt, and pepper.
2. Add chicken slices and marinate for at least 30 minutes.
3. Heat a grill pan or skillet and cook chicken until charred and cooked through.
4. Warm pita bread and assemble shawarma with chicken, veggies, and sauce.
5. Roll up and serve hot.

## Insider Tips

- Use lamb or beef instead of chicken for a different flavor.
- Substitute tahini sauce with yogurt sauce if preferred.

Chicken Shawarma,30

**Normal**

1 serving

45 minutes

# Iraqi Lamb Chops

## Ingredients:

- 2 lamb chops
- 2 tbsp olive oil
- 1 tbsp lemon juice
- 2 cloves garlic, minced
- 1 tsp paprika
- 1 tsp cumin
- 1/2 tsp cinnamon
- Salt and pepper to taste
- Chopped fresh herbs for garnish (parsley, mint)
- Lemon wedges (for serving)

Iraqi Lamb Chops are marinated in a flavorful blend of spices and grilled to perfection, offering a taste of Middle Eastern cuisine at its finest.

## Directions

1. In a bowl, mix olive oil, lemon juice, garlic, paprika, cumin, cinnamon, salt, and pepper.
2. Rub lamb chops with the marinade and let sit for 30 minutes.
3. Preheat grill or grill pan and cook chops until charred and cooked to desired doneness.
4. Garnish with fresh herbs and serve with lemon wedges.

## Insider Tips

- Use beef or chicken chops as a substitute for lamb.
- Adjust spices according to taste preferences.

**1 serving**

**60 minutes**

**Normal**

# Kubba Mosul

## Ingredients:

- 200g ground lamb or beef
- 1/2 cup cracked wheat (burghul), soaked in water
- 1 onion, finely chopped
- 2 cloves garlic, minced
- 1/4 cup chopped parsley
- 1/4 tsp ground allspice
- 1/4 tsp ground cinnamon
- Salt and pepper to taste
- Vegetable oil (for frying)
- Lemon wedges (for serving)

Kubba Mosul, Iraqi stuffed meatballs, are filled with spiced meat and encased in a cracked wheat shell, offering a burst of flavor in every bite.

## Directions

1. Drain soaked cracked wheat and mix with ground meat, onion, garlic, parsley, allspice, cinnamon, salt, and pepper.
2. Form mixture into balls and flatten slightly.
3. Heat oil in a pan and fry kubba until golden and cooked through.
4. Serve hot with lemon wedges.

## Insider Tips

- Use bulgur instead of cracked wheat if needed.
- Add pine nuts or raisins to the meat mixture for extra flavor.

**1 serving**

**120 minutes**

# Iraqi Lamb Stew

## Ingredients:

- 300g lamb chunks
- 1 onion, chopped
- 2 carrots, diced
- 2 potatoes, diced
- 1/2 cup green peas
- 2 cloves garlic, minced
- 1 tsp ground cumin
- 1 tsp ground coriander
- 1/2 tsp cinnamon
- 1/4 tsp turmeric
- Salt and pepper to taste
- Vegetable oil
- Fresh parsley for garnish

Iraqi Lamb Stew, also known as Pacha, is a hearty dish featuring tender lamb cooked with aromatic spices and vegetables, perfect for a comforting meal.

## Directions

1. In a pot, heat oil and sauté onions and garlic until translucent.
2. Add lamb chunks and brown on all sides.
3. Stir in spices and cook until fragrant.
4. Add carrots, potatoes, peas, salt, and pepper.
5. Pour in enough water to cover ingredients.
6. Simmer until lamb and vegetables are tender and sauce is thickened.
7. Adjust seasoning if needed.
8. Serve hot, garnished with fresh parsley.

## Insider Tips

- Use beef or chicken instead of lamb for variation.
- Add chickpeas or beans for extra protein and texture.

**Normal**

1 serving

45 minutes

# Beef Kofta

## Ingredients:

- 200g ground beef
- 1/4 cup breadcrumbs
- 1 egg
- 1/4 cup chopped parsley
- 1/4 cup chopped onion
- 2 cloves garlic, minced
- 1 tsp ground cumin
- 1 tsp ground coriander
- 1/2 tsp paprika
- Salt and pepper to taste
- Olive oil (for grilling)
- Yogurt sauce (mix yogurt with lemon juice, garlic, salt, and pepper)

Beef Kofta, Middle Eastern spiced meatballs, are grilled to perfection and served with a tangy yogurt sauce, offering a burst of flavors in every bite.

## Directions

1. In a bowl, combine ground beef, breadcrumbs, egg, parsley, onion, garlic, cumin, coriander, paprika, salt, and pepper.
2. Mix until well combined and form into kofta shapes.
3. Preheat grill or grill pan and brush with olive oil.
4. Grill kofta until cooked through and charred on the outside.
5. Serve hot with yogurt sauce.

## Insider Tips

- Use lamb or chicken for a different taste.
- Add chopped mint or cilantro to the meat mixture for extra freshness.

# Chapter 4: Main Dishes - Vegetarian

**4 servings**

**45 minutes**

**Normal**

# Iraqi Eggplant and Chickpea Stew

## Ingredients:

1 large eggplant
1 can chickpeas (drained and rinsed)
1 onion (chopped)
2 cloves garlic (minced)
1 can diced tomatoes
1 teaspoon cumin
1 teaspoon paprika
1/2 teaspoon turmeric
salt and pepper to taste

Dive into the heartwarming flavors of Iraqi Eggplant and Chickpea Stew, a culinary journey infused with spices and textures. Originating from the rich heritage of Iraqi cuisine, this stew is a comfort on every spoonful.

## Directions

1. Heat olive oil in a pot over medium heat. Add onion and garlic, sauté until fragrant.
2. Add eggplant, chickpeas, tomatoes, cumin, paprika, turmeric, salt, and pepper.
3. Cover and simmer for 30 minutes or until eggplant is tender.
4. Adjust seasoning if needed. Serve hot.

## Insider Tips

Use canned tomato sauce instead of diced tomatoes.

# Iraqi Style Stuffed Peppers

2 servings

30 minutes

Easy

## Ingredients:

2 large bell peppers
1 cup cooked rice
1/2 lb ground beef or lamb
1 onion (chopped)
2 cloves garlic (minced)
1 teaspoon cumin
1 teaspoon coriander
salt and pepper to taste
tomato sauce for topping

Embark on a culinary adventure with Iraqi Style Stuffed Peppers, where vibrant peppers are filled with a savory blend of rice and spices. A dish steeped in tradition and flavor, perfect for sharing.

## Directions

1. Preheat oven to 375°F (190°C).
2. Cut the tops off the peppers and remove seeds.
3. In a skillet, cook ground meat with onion, garlic, cumin, coriander, salt, and pepper until browned. Mix with cooked rice.
4. Stuff peppers with the meat and rice mixture.
5. Place stuffed peppers in a baking dish, pour tomato sauce over them.
6. Cover with foil and bake for 20-25 minutes. Serve hot.

## Insider Tips

Use ground chicken or turkey for a lighter option.

# Falafel Wrap

## Ingredients:

3 falafel balls
1 large pita bread
lettuce
tomato
cucumber
red onion
tahini sauce

Delight in the flavors of the Middle East with a Falafel Wrap, where crispy falafel balls are nestled in a soft wrap with fresh vegetables and creamy tahini sauce. A handheld delight that's perfect for any meal.

## Directions

1. Warm pita bread in the oven or microwave.
2. Spread tahini sauce on the pita.
3. Place falafel balls and fresh vegetables inside the pita.
4. Wrap it up and enjoy!

## Insider Tips

Add hummus for extra creaminess.

1 serving

25 minutes

Easy

**Normal**

# Stuffed Zucchini (Kousa Mahshi)

4 servings

60 minutes

## Ingredients:

4 medium zucchinis
1 cup cooked rice
1/2 lb ground beef or lamb
1 onion (chopped)
2 cloves garlic (minced)
1/4 cup chopped parsley
1/4 cup chopped mint
salt and pepper to taste
tomato sauce for topping

Experience the comfort of Stuffed Zucchini (Kousa Mahshi), a dish where tender zucchini boats are filled with a flavorful mixture of rice, meat, and herbs. A taste of home in every bite.

## Directions

1. Preheat oven to 375°F (190°C).
2. Cut zucchinis in half lengthwise and scoop out the centers to create boats.
3. In a skillet, cook ground meat with onion, garlic, parsley, mint, salt, and pepper until browned. Mix with cooked rice.
4. Stuff zucchini boats with the meat and rice mixture.
5. Place stuffed zucchinis in a baking dish, pour tomato sauce over them.
6. Cover with foil and bake for 30-35 minutes. Serve hot.

## Insider Tips

Use quinoa instead of rice for a gluten-free option.

# Iraqi Rice and Lentils (Mujaddara)

6 servings

45 minutes

Easy

## Ingredients:

1 cup lentils
1 cup rice
2 onions (sliced)
4 cups water or broth
1 teaspoon cumin
1/2 teaspoon cinnamon
salt and pepper to taste
olive oil for frying onions

Delight in the simplicity and flavor of Iraqi Rice and Lentils (Mujaddara), a comforting dish where rice and lentils are cooked to perfection with caramelized onions. A wholesome meal that's a staple of Iraqi cuisine.

## Directions

1. Rinse lentils and rice separately.
2. In a pot, combine lentils, rice, water or broth, cumin, cinnamon, salt, and pepper. Bring to a boil, then reduce heat and simmer until rice and lentils are cooked (about 25-30 minutes).
3. In a separate pan, heat olive oil and fry sliced onions until golden and crispy.
4. Serve Mujaddara topped with fried onions. Enjoy!

## Insider Tips

Use brown lentils for a firmer texture.

**Normal**

# Spinach and Feta Fatayer

~~~~~~~~~~~~~~~~

## Ingredients:

- 2 cups all-purpose flour
- 1/2 cup warm water
- 1/4 cup olive oil
- 1 teaspoon salt
- 1 cup chopped spinach
- 1/2 cup crumbled feta cheese
- 1/4 cup chopped onions
- 2 tablespoons olive oil
- Salt and pepper to taste

1 serving

45 minutes

A savory Middle Eastern pastry filled with a delightful combination of spinach and creamy feta cheese. Fatayer has its roots in the Levant region, where it is a beloved snack enjoyed with tea or as part of a mezze spread.

## Directions

1. In a bowl, combine flour, warm water, olive oil, and salt. Knead until a smooth dough forms.
2. Cover and let the dough rest for 30 minutes.
3. In a pan, sauté onions in olive oil until translucent. Add spinach and cook until wilted. Season with salt and pepper.
4. Roll out the dough into circles and place a spoonful of the spinach-feta mixture in the center. Fold the dough over the filling and seal the edges.
5. Bake at 350°F (175°C) for 20-25 minutes or until golden brown. 6. Serve warm as a delightful snack or appetizer.

## Insider Tips

- Use ricotta cheese instead of feta
- Add pine nuts or raisins to the filling for variation

# Vegetarian Grape Leaves (Yalanji)

1 serving

60 minutes

## Ingredients:

- 1 jar grape leaves
- 1 cup cooked rice
- 1/4 cup chopped parsley
- 1/4 cup chopped mint
- 1/4 cup chopped onions
- 2 tablespoons olive oil
- 2 tablespoons lemon juice
- Salt and pepper to taste

## Insider Tips

- Use quinoa or bulgur instead of rice
- Add pine nuts or currants to the filling for extra texture

**Normal**

Tender grape leaves stuffed with a flavorful mixture of rice, herbs, and spices, creating a vegetarian delight. Yalanji is a traditional dish in the Levant region, cherished for its tangy and aromatic flavors.

## Directions

1. Drain grape leaves and rinse under cold water.
2. In a bowl, mix cooked rice, parsley, mint, onions, olive oil, lemon juice, salt, and pepper.
3. Place a spoonful of the rice mixture on each grape leaf and roll tightly.
4. Arrange stuffed grape leaves in a pot, layering them neatly.
5. Add water to cover the grape leaves, then place a plate on top to keep them in place.
6. Simmer on low heat for 40-45 minutes or until rice is tender.
7. Serve hot or cold as a delightful appetizer or side dish.

1 serving

40 minutes

# Iraqi Style Lentil Pilaf

**Normal**

A hearty and flavorful pilaf made with lentils, rice, and aromatic spices, inspired by Iraqi cuisine. This dish is a comforting meal that celebrates the earthy flavors of the Middle East.

## Ingredients:

- 1/2 cup lentils, rinsed and drained
- 1/2 cup basmati rice
- 1 cup vegetable broth
- 1/4 cup chopped onions
- 2 cloves garlic, minced
- 1 teaspoon ground cumin
- 1 teaspoon ground coriander
- 1/2 teaspoon turmeric
- Salt and pepper to taste
- 2 tablespoons olive oil

## Directions

1. In a pot, heat olive oil over medium heat.
2. Sauté onions and garlic until golden.
3. Add lentils, rice, cumin, coriander, turmeric, salt, and pepper.
4. Stir to coat the grains with spices.
5. Pour in vegetable broth and bring to a boil.
6. Reduce heat, cover, and simmer for 20-25 minutes or until rice and lentils are tender.
7. Fluff with a fork before serving.

## Insider Tips

- Add chopped tomatoes or bell peppers for extra flavor
- Use chicken broth instead of vegetable broth

# Eggplant Moussaka

A classic Mediterranean dish featuring layers of eggplant, spiced meat sauce, and creamy béchamel sauce, baked to perfection. Moussaka has Greek and Middle Eastern origins, loved for its rich and comforting flavors.

## Ingredients:

- 1 large eggplant, sliced
- 1/2 pound ground lamb or beef
- 1/4 cup chopped onions
- 2 cloves garlic, minced
- 1 teaspoon ground cinnamon
- 1/2 teaspoon ground allspice
- 1 cup tomato sauce
- Salt and pepper to taste
- 2 tablespoons olive oil
- 2 tablespoons butter
- 2 tablespoons all-purpose flour
- 1 cup milk
- 1/4 cup grated Parmesan cheese

## Directions

1. Preheat oven to 375°F (190°C).
2. Arrange eggplant slices on a baking sheet, drizzle with olive oil, and bake for 20-25 minutes or until tender.
3. In a pan, cook ground meat with onions, garlic, cinnamon, allspice, salt, and pepper until browned. Stir in tomato sauce.
4. In another pan, melt butter, stir in flour, and cook until golden. Gradually whisk in milk until thickened. Stir in Parmesan cheese.
5. In a baking dish, layer eggplant, meat sauce, and béchamel sauce. Repeat layers.
6. Bake for 30-35 minutes or until bubbly and golden.
7. Let it rest before serving.

## Insider Tips

- Use ground turkey or tofu for a vegetarian version
- Add a layer of sliced potatoes for extra heartiness

# Stuffed Cabbage Rolls (Malfouf)

2 servings

45 minutes

Discover the heartwarming flavors of Stuffed Cabbage Rolls, a cherished Middle Eastern delight! This recipe's popularity stems from its blend of tender cabbage leaves wrapped around a savory filling, creating a culinary symphony that captivates palates across generations.

## Ingredients:

- 1 large head of cabbage, cored and leaves separated
- 1 cup cooked rice
- 1/2 pound ground beef
- 1/2 onion, finely chopped
- 2 cloves garlic, minced
- 1 teaspoon ground cumin
- 1 teaspoon paprika
- Salt and pepper to taste
- 1 can (14 ounces) tomato sauce
- 1/2 cup chicken broth
- 1 tablespoon olive oil

## Directions

1. Preheat the oven to 350°F (175°C).
2. In a large pot of boiling water, blanch the cabbage leaves until tender, about 5 minutes. Remove and drain.
3. In a skillet, heat olive oil over medium heat. Add onions and garlic, sauté until translucent.
4. Add ground beef, cumin, paprika, salt, and pepper. Cook until beef is browned.
5. Stir in cooked rice and mix well.
6. Place a spoonful of the filling onto each cabbage leaf, roll tightly, and place seam side down in a baking dish.
7. In a bowl, mix tomato sauce and chicken broth. Pour over the cabbage rolls.
8. Cover the dish with foil and bake for 30 minutes.
9. Uncover and bake for an additional 10 minutes until the sauce is bubbly.
10. Serve hot and enjoy the comforting flavors of Stuffed Cabbage Rolls!

## Insider Tips

- Ground turkey or chicken can be substituted for beef.<br>- Brown rice can be used instead of white rice.<br>- Vegetable broth can replace chicken broth.<br>- Add chopped herbs like parsley or dill for extra freshness.

# Chapter 5:
# Rice and Grains

1 serving

30 minutes

Easy

# Iraqi Yellow Rice (Timman)

## Ingredients:

- 1 cup basmati rice
- 2 cups water
- 1 tbsp butter
- 1/2 tsp turmeric
- Salt to taste
- Chopped parsley for garnish

Iraqi Yellow Rice, known as Timman, is a fragrant and flavorful rice dish from Iraq. Its golden hue comes from turmeric, and it's often served alongside grilled meats or stews, adding vibrancy to the meal.

## Directions

1. Rinse rice under cold water until water runs clear.
2. In a saucepan, melt butter and add turmeric, stirring for 1 minute.
3. Add rice and water. Bring to a boil, then reduce heat and cover.
4. Simmer for 18-20 minutes until rice is tender and water is absorbed.
5. Fluff with a fork, garnish with parsley, and serve hot.

## Insider Tips

- Saffron can be used instead of turmeric for a richer flavor and color.
- Olive oil can replace butter for a dairy-free version.

# Iraqi Chicken Machboos

~~~~~~~~~~~~~~~~

## Ingredients:

- 1 lb chicken pieces
- 1 cup basmati rice
- 2 cups chicken broth
- 1 onion, chopped
- 2 tomatoes, chopped
- 2 cloves garlic, minced
- 1 tsp cinnamon
- 1/2 tsp cardamom
- 1/4 tsp cloves
- Salt and pepper to taste
- Chopped cilantro for garnish

1 serving

60 minutes

Normal

Iraqi Chicken Machboos is a traditional rice and chicken dish from Iraq. It's infused with aromatic spices like cinnamon, cardamom, and cloves, creating a comforting and hearty meal loved by many.

## Directions

1. In a pot, brown chicken pieces. Remove and sauté onion, garlic, and spices.
2. Add tomatoes, chicken broth, and chicken back to the pot.
3. Simmer until chicken is cooked and tender.
4. Remove chicken, add rice to the broth, and cook until tender.
5. Serve rice topped with chicken, garnished with cilantro.

## Insider Tips

- Lamb can be used instead of chicken for a different flavor.
- Ras el Hanout spice blend can replace individual spices.

**Hard**

# Maqluba (Upside-Down Rice)

~~~~~~~~~~~~~~~~

1 serving

90 minutes

## Ingredients:

- 1 cup basmati rice
- 1 lb chicken or lamb, cubed
- 2 potatoes, sliced
- 1 eggplant, sliced
- 1 onion, sliced
- 2 tomatoes, sliced
- 1/2 cup peas
- 1 tsp cumin
- 1 tsp paprika
- Salt and pepper to taste
- Chopped parsley for garnish

Maqluba, meaning "upside-down" in Arabic, is a traditional Middle Eastern dish enjoyed in Iraq. It features layers of rice, vegetables, and meat, cooked together and then flipped upside down for a stunning presentation.

## Directions

1. Brown meat in a pot. Remove and sauté onions, then layer potatoes, eggplant, tomatoes, and peas.
2. Season with spices, salt, and pepper.
3. Add rice on top, then meat. Pour water to cover.
4. Simmer until rice and meat are cooked.
5. Invert the pot onto a serving plate, garnish with parsley, and serve hot.

## Insider Tips

- Cauliflower can replace potatoes for a low-carb version.
- Any meat or vegetable can be used based on preference.

# Iraqi Rice Pilaf with Vermicelli

## Ingredients:

- 1 cup basmati rice
- 1/2 cup vermicelli noodles
- 2 cups chicken or vegetable broth
- 2 tbsp butter
- Salt and pepper to taste
- Chopped parsley for garnish

**1 serving**

**45 minutes**

**Easy**

Iraqi Rice Pilaf with Vermicelli is a classic side dish in Iraqi cuisine. It combines fluffy rice with toasted vermicelli noodles, creating a textural delight that pairs well with a variety of main dishes.

## Directions

1. In a pan, toast vermicelli in butter until golden. Add rice and sauté briefly.
2. Pour broth over rice, season with salt and pepper.
3. Bring to a boil, then cover and simmer until rice is cooked.
4. Fluff with a fork, garnish with parsley, and serve hot.

## Insider Tips

- Orzo pasta can be used instead of vermicelli for a similar texture.
- Olive oil can replace butter for a vegan option.

**1 serving**

**25 minutes**

# Iraqi Style Quinoa Pilaf

## Ingredients:

- 1 cup quinoa
- 1 3/4 cups water or broth
- 1 onion, diced
- 1 carrot, diced
- 1/2 cup peas
- 1 tsp cumin
- 1 tsp coriander
- Salt and pepper to taste
- Chopped mint for garnish

**Easy**

Iraqi Style Quinoa Pilaf is a modern twist on a traditional dish, incorporating nutritious quinoa with Middle Eastern flavors. It's a wholesome and satisfying meal that's both delicious and healthy.

## Directions

1. Rinse quinoa under cold water. In a pot, sauté onion and carrot until softened.
2. Add quinoa, water or broth, and spices. Bring to a boil.
3. Reduce heat, cover, and simmer until quinoa is cooked and liquid is absorbed.
4. Stir in peas, season with salt and pepper.
5. Garnish with chopped mint and serve warm.

## Insider Tips

- Any vegetables like bell peppers or zucchini can be added for variation.
- Use any herbs like parsley or cilantro if mint is unavailable.

**1 serving**

**20 minutes**

# Bulgur Wheat Salad (Tabbouleh)

**Easy**

Tabbouleh, a refreshing Bulgur Wheat Salad, originates from the Levantine region and is cherished for its vibrant flavors. Did you know? Tabbouleh was traditionally made with more herbs than bulgur, emphasizing freshness and healthiness.

## Ingredients:

- 1/2 cup bulgur wheat
- 1 cup boiling water
- 1 cup chopped parsley
- 1/2 cup chopped mint
- 1/2 cup diced tomatoes
- 1/4 cup finely chopped red onion
- 1/4 cup lemon juice
- 1/4 cup olive oil
- Salt and pepper to taste
- Optional: cucumber, chopped
- Optional: feta cheese, crumbled
- Optional: black olives

## Directions

1. Place bulgur wheat in a bowl and cover with boiling water. Let it sit for 15-20 minutes or until softened.
2. Fluff the bulgur with a fork and let it cool.
3. In a large bowl, combine chopped parsley, mint, tomatoes, red onion, and optional cucumber.
4. Add the cooled bulgur to the bowl and mix well.
5. In a small bowl, whisk together lemon juice, olive oil, salt, and pepper.
6. Pour the dressing over the salad and toss to combine.
7. Optional: Add crumbled feta cheese and black olives for extra flavor.
8. Chill the Tabbouleh in the refrigerator before serving.

## Insider Tips

- Use quinoa or couscous instead of bulgur wheat.
- Substitute lime juice for lemon juice.
- Add diced bell peppers for color and crunch.
- Omit feta cheese for a vegan version.

# Iraqi Rice with Mixed Vegetables

Iraqi Rice with Mixed Vegetables is a hearty and flavorful dish that reflects the culinary diversity of Iraq. It's popular for family gatherings and special occasions, showcasing a harmonious blend of spices and textures. A fun fact about this dish is that each region in Iraq has its unique variation, adding a touch of regional pride to the recipe.

1 serving

30 minutes

## Ingredients:

- 1 cup basmati rice
- 2 cups water
- 1 tablespoon olive oil
- 1/2 cup chopped onions
- 1/2 cup mixed vegetables (carrots, peas, corn)
- 1/4 teaspoon cumin powder
- 1/4 teaspoon paprika
- Salt and pepper to taste
- Fresh parsley for garnish
- Optional: toasted pine nuts

## Directions

1. Rinse basmati rice until the water runs clear, then drain.
2. In a saucepan, heat olive oil and sauté chopped onions until translucent.
3. Add mixed vegetables and sauté until slightly tender.
4. Stir in cumin powder, paprika, salt, and pepper.
5. Add rinsed rice to the saucepan and sauté for 2-3 minutes.
6. Pour water into the saucepan and bring to a boil.
7. Reduce heat to low, cover, and simmer for 15-20 minutes or until rice is cooked and water is absorbed.
8. Fluff the rice with a fork and garnish with fresh parsley and toasted pine nuts.
9. Serve hot as a flavorful side dish or main course.

## Insider Tips

- Use jasmine rice or long-grain rice instead of basmati.
- Substitute mixed vegetables with your favorite veggies like bell peppers or broccoli.
- Add raisins or dried cranberries for a sweet contrast.
- Garnish with chopped cilantro if parsley is not available.

1 serving

40 minutes

# Lentil and Rice Pilaf (Mujaddara)

## Ingredients:

- 1/2 cup brown lentils
- 1/2 cup basmati rice
- 1 cup water
- 2 tablespoons olive oil
- 1 large onion, thinly sliced
- 1 teaspoon cumin seeds
- 1 teaspoon coriander powder
- Salt and pepper to taste
- Fresh cilantro for garnish
- Optional: yogurt for serving

Mujaddara, a comforting Lentil and Rice Pilaf, has been a staple dish in Middle Eastern cuisine for centuries. Its humble ingredients of lentils, rice, and caramelized onions create a satisfying and nutritious meal. Did you know? Mujaddara is often associated with the Prophet Muhammad, who praised its simplicity and wholesome flavor.

## Directions

1. Rinse brown lentils and basmati rice separately, then drain.
2. In a saucepan, combine lentils and water. Bring to a boil, then reduce heat and simmer for 15-20 minutes or until lentils are tender.
3. In another saucepan, heat olive oil and sauté thinly sliced onion until golden brown and caramelized.
4. Add cumin seeds and coriander powder to the onions, sauté for 1 minute.
5. Add cooked lentils and rice to the onion mixture. Season with salt and pepper.
6. Cover and cook over low heat for 15-20 minutes or until rice is fluffy and fully cooked.
7. Fluff the Mujaddara with a fork and garnish with fresh cilantro.
8. Serve hot with a dollop of yogurt if desired.

## Insider Tips

- Use green or black lentils for a different texture.
- Substitute basmati rice with brown rice for added nuttiness.
- Add a pinch of cinnamon or allspice for extra flavor.
- Top with toasted almonds or pine nuts for a crunchy contrast.

**1 serving**

**30 minutes**

**Easy**

# Couscous with Roasted Vegetables

## Ingredients:

1/2 cup couscous
1 cup water or vegetable broth
1 bell pepper (sliced)
1 zucchini (sliced)
1 red onion (sliced)
2 tablespoons olive oil
1 teaspoon cumin
1 teaspoon paprika
Salt and pepper to taste
Fresh parsley for garnish

## Insider Tips

Use any vegetables of your choice for roasting.

Couscous with Roasted Vegetables is a delightful fusion of Mediterranean flavors and Middle Eastern flair. Originating from the sun-kissed shores of North Africa, this dish has gained popularity worldwide for its vibrant colors, robust taste, and effortless preparation. It's a harmonious blend of fluffy couscous, caramelized vegetables, and a burst of aromatic herbs and spices, making it a go-to option for quick and satisfying meals.

## Directions

1. Preheat the oven to 400°F (200°C). Toss the sliced vegetables with olive oil, cumin, paprika, salt, and pepper on a baking sheet. Roast for 20-25 minutes or until tender and slightly caramelized.
2. Meanwhile, prepare the couscous according to package instructions using water or broth.
3. Fluff the couscous with a fork and top it with the roasted vegetables.
4. Garnish with fresh parsley and serve hot or at room temperature.

1 serving

40 minutes

# Iraqi Rice with Dried Fruits and Nuts

Normal

## Ingredients:

1/2 cup basmati rice
1 cup water or vegetable broth
1/4 cup mixed dried fruits (such as raisins, apricots, and cranberries)
1/4 cup mixed nuts (such as almonds, pistachios, and cashews)
1 tablespoon butter or olive oil
1 teaspoon cinnamon
Salt to taste
Fresh parsley for garnish

## Insider Tips

Use quinoa or bulgur for a gluten-free option.
Use ghee instead of butter for a richer flavor.

Iraqi Rice with Dried Fruits and Nuts is a celebratory dish that embodies the richness and hospitality of Iraqi cuisine. This aromatic and flavorful rice dish is adorned with a symphony of dried fruits and nuts, creating a delightful texture and a burst of sweetness in every bite. Originating from traditional Iraqi feasts, this recipe has been cherished for generations, symbolizing prosperity, abundance, and the joy of communal dining.

## Directions

1. Rinse the rice under cold water until the water runs clear. In a pot, combine the rice, water or broth, dried fruits, nuts, butter or olive oil, cinnamon, and salt.
2. Bring to a boil, then reduce heat to low. Cover and simmer for 15-20 minutes or until the rice is tender and the liquid is absorbed.
3. Fluff the rice with a fork and let it rest for 5 minutes.
4. Garnish with fresh parsley and serve hot as a side dish or main course.

# We have a small favor to ask

As we delve into "The Iraqi Home Cook," we're excited to have you join us for an immersive experience into Iraqi gastronomy!

Now, let's keep it real. We're just passionate cooks, not culinary experts. If you spot any tiny slip-ups, please forgive us. We're all about learning and improving our kitchen skills!

Your review is the secret ingredient. As a small publisher, your feedback can truly shape the success of our cookbook. Share your thoughts, and let's make this cookbook as delightful as the flavors of Iraq!

Now, let's get back to cooking up some Middle Eastern delights. It's time to savor the rich and diverse dishes of Iraq and embark on a culinary journey like no other!

Warm regards,

# Chapter 6:
# Breads and Pastries

1 serving

90 minutes

# Iraqi Khubz Bread

## Ingredients:

- 3 cups all-purpose flour
- 1 cup warm water
- 1 tbsp active dry yeast
- 1 tsp sugar
- 1 tsp salt
- Olive oil for brushing
- Sesame seeds for garnish

Enjoy the authentic taste of Iraqi Khubz Bread, a traditional flatbread that's soft and fluffy, perfect for savoring with stews or as a wrap for your favorite fillings.

## Directions

1. Dissolve yeast and sugar in warm water, let it activate for 10 minutes.
2. In a large bowl, combine flour and salt.
3. Pour in yeast mixture, knead into a smooth dough.
4. Cover and let rise for 1 hour.
5. Preheat oven to 400°F (200°C).
6. Divide dough into balls, flatten into rounds.
7. Brush with olive oil, sprinkle with sesame seeds.
8. Bake for 10-12 minutes until golden.
9. Serve warm.
10. Enjoy the homemade goodness!

## Insider Tips

- Use whole wheat flour for a healthier option.

**1 serving**

**60 minutes**

# Iraqi Sweet Bread (Kleicha)

## Ingredients:

- 2 cups all-purpose flour
- 1/2 cup warm milk
- 1/4 cup sugar
- 1/4 cup butter, melted
- 1 tsp active dry yeast
- 1/2 tsp ground cardamom
- 1/2 tsp vanilla extract
- Pinch of salt
- Date paste or chopped nuts
- Powdered sugar for dusting

## Insider Tips

- Use honey instead of sugar for a natural sweetness.

**Normal**

Delight in the sweetness of Iraqi Sweet Bread (Kleicha), a traditional pastry filled with dates or nuts, baked to golden perfection and sprinkled with powdered sugar.

## Directions

1. Dissolve yeast and sugar in warm milk, let it activate for 10 minutes.
2. In a bowl, combine flour, melted butter, cardamom, vanilla extract, and salt.
3. Pour in yeast mixture, knead into a soft dough.
4. Cover and let rise for 30 minutes.
5. Preheat oven to 350°F (175°C).
6. Roll out dough, spread date paste or nuts, roll into a log.
7. Cut into pieces, place on a baking sheet.
8. Bake for 15-20 minutes until golden.
9. Dust with powdered sugar.
10. Serve and savor the delightful flavors.

Normal

# Iraqi Cheese Borek

1 serving

45 minutes

## Ingredients:

- 1 package phyllo dough
- 1 cup feta cheese, crumbled
- 1 cup mozzarella cheese, shredded
- 1/4 cup fresh parsley, chopped
- 1/4 cup fresh dill, chopped
- 1/4 cup olive oil
- Salt and pepper to taste
- Egg wash (1 egg + 1 tbsp water)

## Insider Tips

- Use other types of cheese for variety.

Indulge in the savory delight of Iraqi Cheese Borek, crispy pastry filled with a blend of cheeses and herbs, perfect for a flavorful snack or appetizer.

## Directions

1. Preheat oven to 375°F (190°C).
2. In a bowl, mix feta cheese, mozzarella cheese, parsley, dill, olive oil, salt, and pepper.
3. Lay out a sheet of phyllo dough, brush with egg wash.
4. Place a spoonful of cheese mixture on the dough, fold into triangles.
5. Repeat with remaining dough and filling.
6. Brush triangles with egg wash, sprinkle with sesame seeds if desired.
7. Bake for 20-25 minutes until golden and crisp.
8. Serve warm and enjoy the cheesy goodness!

1 serving

60 minutes

# Za'atar Flatbread

## Ingredients:

- 2 cups all-purpose flour
- 1 cup warm water
- 1 tbsp active dry yeast
- 1 tbsp olive oil
- 1 tbsp za'atar seasoning
- 1 tsp sugar
- 1/2 tsp salt
- Olive oil for brushing

## Insider Tips

- Add minced garlic for extra flavor.

Delve into the aromatic flavors of Za'atar Flatbread, a Middle Eastern-inspired delight topped with a blend of herbs, spices, and olive oil, perfect for a snack or side dish.

## Directions

1. Dissolve yeast and sugar in warm water, let it activate for 10 minutes.
2. In a bowl, combine flour, olive oil, salt, and activated yeast mixture.
3. Knead into a smooth dough.
4. Cover and let rise for 30 minutes.
5. Preheat oven to 400°F (200°C).
6. Divide dough into balls, flatten into rounds.
7. Brush with olive oil, sprinkle with za'atar seasoning.
8. Bake for 15-20 minutes until golden.
9. Serve warm and enjoy the aromatic flavors.
10. Perfect for dipping in olive oil or hummus.

**1 serving**

**75 minutes**

# Iraqi Date Bread (Khubz Tamr)

## Ingredients:

- 2 cups all-purpose flour
- 1 cup warm water
- 1/2 cup chopped dates
- 1/4 cup honey
- 1 tbsp active dry yeast
- 1 tbsp olive oil
- 1 tsp ground cinnamon
- 1/2 tsp ground cardamom
- 1/2 tsp salt
- Olive oil for brushing

## Insider Tips

- Use maple syrup instead of honey for a different flavor.

**Normal**

Experience the sweetness of Iraqi Date Bread (Khubz Tamr), a traditional bread infused with dates, honey, and spices, offering a delightful treat for any occasion.

## Directions

1. Dissolve yeast and honey in warm water, let it activate for 10 minutes.
2. In a bowl, mix flour, chopped dates, olive oil, cinnamon, cardamom, and salt.
3. Pour in activated yeast mixture, knead into a soft dough.
4. Cover and let rise for 1 hour.
5. Preheat oven to 375°F (190°C).
6. Divide dough into balls, flatten into rounds.
7. Brush with olive oil, make slight indentations with fingers.
8. Bake for 15-20 minutes until golden.
9. Serve warm and enjoy the delicious sweetness.

# Iraqi Spinach Turnovers

1 serving

60 minutes

Easy

## Ingredients:

- 1 lb fresh spinach (chopped)
- 1 onion (chopped)
- 2 cloves garlic (minced)
- 1/2 cup feta cheese (crumbled)
- 1/4 cup olive oil
- Salt and pepper to taste
- 1 package puff pastry (thawed)
- Egg wash (1 egg beaten with a splash of water)
- Sesame seeds (for topping)

Iraqi Spinach Turnovers are savory pastries filled with a delightful spinach mixture, perfect for a tasty snack or appetizer.

## Directions

1. Sauté chopped onion and minced garlic in olive oil until softened.
2. Add chopped spinach and cook until wilted. Season with salt and pepper.
3. Remove from heat and stir in crumbled feta cheese.
4. Cut puff pastry into squares, place spinach mixture in the center, fold over, and seal edges.
5. Brush with egg wash, sprinkle with sesame seeds, and bake until golden brown.
6. Serve warm.

## Insider Tips

Use ricotta cheese instead of feta for a milder flavor.

# Iraqi Potato Bread

⎯⎯⎯⎯⎯⎯⎯⎯⎯⎯

**1 serving**

**90 minutes**

**Normal**

## Ingredients:

- 2 cups all-purpose flour
- 1/2 cup mashed potatoes
- 1/4 cup olive oil
- 1 tsp yeast
- 1 tsp sugar
- 1/2 tsp salt
- Warm water
- Sesame seeds (for topping, optional)

Iraqi Potato Bread is a soft and fluffy bread made with mashed potatoes, perfect for sandwiches or to accompany any meal.

## Directions

1. Mix flour, mashed potatoes, olive oil, yeast, sugar, and salt in a bowl.
2. Gradually add warm water to form a dough.
3. Knead dough until smooth and elastic.
4. Cover and let rise until doubled in size.
5. Shape dough into loaves or rolls, sprinkle with sesame seeds if using.
6. Bake until golden brown.
7. Enjoy fresh and warm.

## Insider Tips

Use butter instead of olive oil for a richer flavor.

**Normal**

1 serving

45 minutes

# Cheese Sambousek

## Ingredients:

- 2 cups all-purpose flour
- 1/2 cup butter (softened)
- 1/2 cup yogurt
- 1/2 tsp baking powder
- 1/2 tsp salt
- Filling: 1 cup shredded cheese (such as feta or mozzarella)
- 1 egg (beaten)
- Sesame seeds (for topping)

Cheese Sambousek is a delightful Iraqi pastry filled with a cheesy mixture, perfect for a savory snack or appetizer.

## Directions

1. Mix flour, softened butter, yogurt, baking powder, and salt in a bowl to form a dough.
2. Roll out dough and cut into circles.
3. Place a spoonful of cheese filling in the center of each circle.
4. Fold over to form a half-moon shape, seal edges, and crimp with a fork.
5. Brush with beaten egg, sprinkle with sesame seeds, and bake until golden brown.
6. Serve warm and enjoy the cheesy goodness.

## Insider Tips

Use different types of cheese for a variety of flavors.

**1 serving**

**75 minutes**

Normal

# Iraqi Onion Bread

## Ingredients:

- 3 cups all-purpose flour
- 1 onion (finely chopped)
- 1/4 cup olive oil
- 1 tsp yeast
- 1 tsp sugar
- 1/2 tsp salt
- Warm water
- Fresh parsley (chopped, for garnish)
- Sesame seeds (for topping, optional)

Iraqi Onion Bread is a flavorful flatbread infused with onions, perfect for dipping or as a side dish to complement meals.

## Directions

1. Sauté finely chopped onion in olive oil until translucent. Let cool.
2. Mix flour, sautéed onion, yeast, sugar, and salt in a bowl.
3. Gradually add warm water to form a dough.
4. Knead until smooth and elastic.
5. Cover and let rise until doubled in size.
6. Divide dough into portions, shape into rounds, sprinkle with sesame seeds if using.
7. Bake until golden brown.
8. Garnish with chopped parsley before serving.

## Insider Tips

Add garlic powder or herbs to the dough for extra flavor.

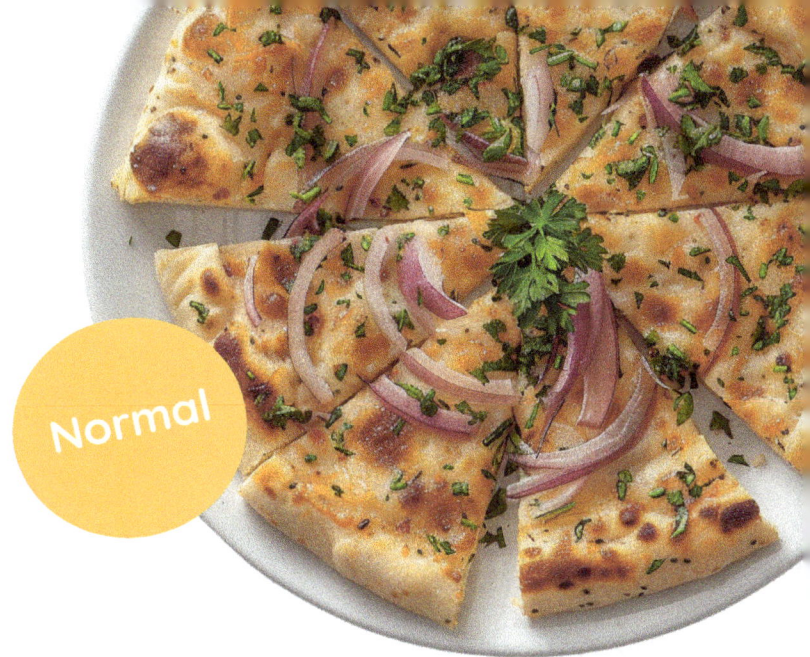

# Iraqi Sesame Cookies

## Ingredients:

- 2 cups all-purpose flour
- 1/2 cup butter (softened)
- 1/2 cup sugar
- 1 egg
- 1 tsp vanilla extract
- 1/2 tsp ground cardamom
- 1/4 tsp salt
- Sesame seeds (for coating)
- Optional: date paste or nuts for filling

Iraqi Sesame Cookies, known as Kleicha Simsim, are delicate and aromatic treats made with sesame seeds and spices.

## Directions

1. Cream softened butter and sugar until light and fluffy.
2. Add egg, vanilla extract, cardamom, and salt. Mix well.
3. Gradually add flour and knead until dough forms.
4. Roll dough into balls, flatten slightly, and make an indentation in the center.
5. Fill with date paste or nuts if desired.
6. Roll in sesame seeds to coat.
7. Place on a baking sheet and bake until golden around the edges.
8. Let cool before enjoying these aromatic cookies.

## Insider Tips

Use almond or coconut flour for a gluten-free option.

# Chapter 7:
# Salads and Sides

1 serving

15 minutes

**Super Easy**

# Iraqi Cucumber Salad

## Ingredients:

- 1 cucumber, thinly sliced
- 1/4 red onion, thinly sliced
- 1/4 cup fresh parsley, chopped
- 1/4 cup fresh mint, chopped
- 1 tbsp lemon juice
- 2 tbsp olive oil
- Salt and pepper to taste
- Optional: cherry tomatoes for garnish

Iraqi Cucumber Salad is a refreshing dish featuring crisp cucumbers, tangy lemon, and aromatic herbs, perfect as a side or light meal.

## Directions

1. In a bowl, combine cucumber slices, red onion, parsley, mint, lemon juice, olive oil, salt, and pepper.
2. Toss well to coat evenly.
3. Garnish with cherry tomatoes if desired.
4. Serve chilled as a refreshing salad or side dish.

## Insider Tips

- Use dill instead of mint for a different flavor.
- Add crumbled feta cheese for extra richness.

**1 serving**

**30 minutes**

# Iraqi Beetroot Salad

## Ingredients:

- 1 medium beetroot, boiled and diced
- 1/4 cup plain yogurt
- 1 tbsp lemon juice
- 1/4 cup walnuts, chopped
- 1 tbsp olive oil
- Salt and pepper to taste
- Fresh parsley for garnish

**Easy**

Iraqi Beetroot Salad is a vibrant and nutritious dish featuring earthy beets, tangy yogurt, and crunchy walnuts, perfect for a colorful meal.

## Directions

1. In a bowl, mix boiled and diced beetroot with yogurt, lemon juice, olive oil, salt, and pepper.
2. Toss in chopped walnuts and parsley.
3. Adjust seasoning if needed.
4. Serve chilled as a nutritious and colorful salad.

## Insider Tips

- Use Greek yogurt for a creamier texture.
- Substitute walnuts with almonds or pecans if preferred.

**1 serving**

**10 minutes**

# Tamarind Salad Dressing

## Ingredients:

- 2 tbsp tamarind paste
- 1 tbsp honey
- 1 tbsp olive oil
- 1/2 tsp ground cumin
- 1/2 tsp paprika
- Salt and pepper to taste

**Easy**

Tamarind Salad Dressing adds a zesty and tangy kick to salads, combining sweet tamarind with savory spices for a flavorful dressing.

## Directions

1. In a small bowl, whisk together tamarind paste, honey, olive oil, cumin, paprika, salt, and pepper until well combined.
2. Adjust sweetness and seasoning to taste.
3. Drizzle over salads just before serving for a burst of flavor.

## Insider Tips

- Use maple syrup or agave nectar instead of honey.
- Add a pinch of chili powder for a spicy version.

**1 serving**

**30 minutes**

**Easy**

# Iraqi Potato Salad

## Ingredients:

- 2 potatoes, boiled and diced
- 1/4 cup mayonnaise
- 1 tbsp mustard
- 1/4 cup chopped celery
- 1/4 cup chopped pickles
- Salt and pepper to taste
- Optional: chopped parsley for garnish

Iraqi Potato Salad is a creamy and comforting dish featuring tender potatoes, crunchy veggies, and a tangy dressing, perfect for picnics and gatherings.

## Directions

1. In a bowl, combine boiled and diced potatoes with mayonnaise, mustard, celery, pickles, salt, and pepper.
2. Mix until potatoes are coated evenly.
3. Garnish with chopped parsley if desired.
4. Chill in the refrigerator before serving for enhanced flavor.

## Insider Tips

- Use Greek yogurt instead of mayonnaise for a healthier option.
- Add chopped hard-boiled eggs for extra protein.

**1 serving**

**20 minutes**

# Iraqi Tomato Salad

## Ingredients:

- 2 tomatoes, diced
- 1/2 cucumber, diced
- 1/4 red onion, thinly sliced
- 1 tbsp lemon juice
- 2 tbsp olive oil
- Salt and pepper to taste
- Fresh basil leaves for garnish

**Easy**

Iraqi Tomato Salad is a simple yet flavorful dish featuring ripe tomatoes, crisp cucumbers, and a zesty lemon dressing, perfect for a quick and refreshing side.

## Directions

1. In a bowl, combine diced tomatoes, cucumber, red onion, lemon juice, olive oil, salt, and pepper.
2. Toss well to coat evenly.
3. Garnish with fresh basil leaves.
4. Serve immediately as a refreshing side salad.

## Insider Tips

- Use balsamic vinegar instead of lemon juice for a different tanginess.
- Add crumbled feta cheese for extra richness.

1 Serving     15 minutes

# Iraqi Coleslaw

## Ingredients:

1 cup shredded cabbage
1/2 cup shredded carrots
2 tablespoons chopped fresh parsley
1/4 cup mayonnaise
1 tablespoon lemon juice
Salt and pepper to taste

**Easy**

A Refreshing Twist
This Iraqi Coleslaw adds a delightful Middle Eastern flair to any meal. With its crunchy cabbage and vibrant flavors, it's a perfect side dish for picnics or barbecues.
Fun Fact: Coleslaw originated from the Dutch term "koolsla," which means "cabbage salad." It has evolved over centuries and is now enjoyed worldwide in various culinary styles.

## Directions

1. In a large bowl, combine shredded cabbage, shredded carrots, and chopped parsley.
2. In a separate bowl, whisk together mayonnaise, lemon juice, salt, and pepper to make the dressing.
3. Pour the dressing over the cabbage mixture and toss until evenly coated.
4. Chill the coleslaw in the refrigerator for at least 30 minutes before serving.
5. Serve chilled as a refreshing side dish.

## Insider Tips

- Use Greek yogurt instead of mayonnaise for a lighter option.
- Add a pinch of cumin or paprika for extra flavor.
- Include diced apples or raisins for a touch of sweetness.

1 Serving

20 minutes

# Pickled Turnips (Shamandar)

## Ingredients:

1 medium turnip (peeled and sliced)
1 cup water
1/2 cup vinegar
2 tablespoons salt
1 tablespoon sugar
1 garlic clove (peeled)
1 teaspoon whole peppercorns

## Insider Tips

- Add beet slices to the pickling liquid for a colorful twist.
- Use apple cider vinegar for a slightly sweeter flavor.
- Include a pinch of turmeric for a golden hue.

Tangy and Vibrant
Pickled Turnips, known as Shamandar in Iraqi cuisine, are a tangy and vibrant addition to any mezze spread. Their refreshing crunch and pickled goodness make them a favorite among Middle Eastern food enthusiasts.
Fun Fact: Pickling is an ancient preservation method used to extend the shelf life of vegetables and add a unique flavor profile.

## Directions

1. In a saucepan, combine water, vinegar, salt, sugar, garlic, and peppercorns. Bring to a boil, then reduce heat and simmer for 5 minutes.
2. Place the sliced turnip in a sterilized jar.
3. Pour the hot pickling liquid over the turnips, ensuring they are completely submerged.
4. Let the pickled turnips cool to room temperature, then seal the jar and refrigerate for at least 24 hours before serving.
5. Enjoy pickled turnips as a tangy and crunchy snack or as part of a mezze platter.

# Iraqi Eggplant Salad

*1 Serving*  *30 minutes*

**Normal**

## Ingredients:

1 large eggplant
2 tablespoons olive oil
Salt and pepper to taste
1/4 cup chopped fresh parsley
2 tablespoons lemon juice
1 garlic clove (minced)
1/4 cup feta cheese (crumbled)

### Mediterranean Delight

This Iraqi Eggplant Salad is a medley of flavors from the Mediterranean region. Roasted eggplant, fresh herbs, and tangy dressing come together to create a refreshing and nutritious dish.

Fun Fact: Eggplants are technically berries and belong to the nightshade family, which also includes tomatoes and potatoes.

## Directions

1. Preheat the oven to 400°F (200°C).
2. Slice the eggplant into rounds, brush with olive oil, and season with salt and pepper.
3. Roast the eggplant in the oven for 20-25 minutes until tender and golden brown.
4. In a bowl, combine chopped parsley, lemon juice, minced garlic, and crumbled feta cheese.
5. Once the eggplant is roasted, let it cool slightly, then chop it into bite-sized pieces.
6. Toss the roasted eggplant with the parsley-feta mixture.
7. Serve the Iraqi Eggplant Salad chilled or at room temperature.

## Insider Tips

- Substitute crumbled goat cheese for feta cheese.
- Add chopped cherry tomatoes for extra freshness.
- Drizzle with balsamic glaze for a touch of sweetness.

**Easy**

# Iraqi Style Tzatziki

## Ingredients:

1 cup Greek yogurt
1/2 cucumber (seeded and grated)
1 garlic clove (minced)
1 tablespoon chopped fresh dill
1 tablespoon olive oil
Salt and pepper to taste

Creamy and Refreshing
Iraqi Style Tzatziki is a creamy yogurt-based dip infused with cucumbers, garlic, and dill. It's a refreshing accompaniment to grilled meats, falafel, or as a dip for pita bread.
Fun Fact: Tzatziki originated in Greece and has become a popular condiment in Mediterranean and Middle Eastern cuisines.

## Directions

1. In a bowl, combine Greek yogurt, grated cucumber, minced garlic, chopped dill, olive oil, salt, and pepper.
2. Mix well until all ingredients are evenly incorporated.
3. Chill the Tzatziki in the refrigerator for at least 30 minutes to allow the flavors to meld.
4. Serve Iraqi Style Tzatziki as a dip or sauce with your favorite dishes.

## Insider Tips

- Use sour cream instead of Greek yogurt for a milder flavor.
- Add a squeeze of lemon juice for extra tanginess.
- Garnish with a sprinkle of paprika or sumac for color.

Easy

# Spicy Carrot Salad

## Ingredients:

2 cups grated carrots
2 tablespoons olive oil
1 tablespoon lemon juice
1 teaspoon honey
1/2 teaspoon cumin
1/4 teaspoon cayenne pepper
Salt and pepper to taste

Zesty and Colorful
Spicy Carrot Salad brings a burst of zesty flavors to the table. With a mix of carrots, herbs, and a touch of heat, it's a perfect side dish to complement any meal.
Fun Fact: Carrots are rich in beta-carotene, which is converted into vitamin A in the body, essential for eye health and immunity.

## Directions

1. In a bowl, whisk together olive oil, lemon juice, honey, cumin, cayenne pepper, salt, and pepper to make the dressing.
2. Add grated carrots to the dressing and toss until evenly coated.
3. Let the salad marinate for at least 10 minutes to allow the flavors to meld.
4. Serve the Spicy Carrot Salad chilled and garnish with fresh herbs if desired.

## Insider Tips

- Substitute lime juice for lemon juice for a tangy twist.
- Use agave syrup instead of honey for a vegan option.
- Add chopped parsley or cilantro for extra freshness.

# Chapter 8: Sauces and Dips

Easy

# Tahini Sauce

## Ingredients:

- 1/2 cup tahini paste
- 1/4 cup water
- 2 tablespoons lemon juice
- 1 clove garlic, minced
- Salt to taste

1 serving

10 minutes

A creamy and nutty sauce made from sesame seeds, perfect for drizzling over salads, falafel, or grilled vegetables. Tahini sauce has been a staple in Middle Eastern cuisine for centuries, loved for its versatility and flavor.

## Directions

1. In a bowl, whisk together tahini paste, water, lemon juice, minced garlic, and salt until smooth.
2. Adjust the consistency with more water if needed.
3. Serve as a dip or sauce.

## Insider Tips

- Use lime juice instead of lemon for a tangier flavor
- Add chopped fresh herbs like parsley or cilantro for freshness

# Garlic Yogurt Sauce (Toum)

## Ingredients:

- 1/2 cup tahini paste
- 1/4 cup water
- 2 tablespoons lemon juice
- 1 clove garlic, minced
- Salt to taste

A creamy and nutty sauce made from sesame seeds, perfect for drizzling over salads, falafel, or grilled vegetables. Tahini sauce has been a staple in Middle Eastern cuisine for centuries, loved for its versatility and flavor.

## Directions

1. In a bowl, whisk together tahini paste, water, lemon juice, minced garlic, and salt until smooth.
2. Adjust the consistency with more water if needed.
3. Serve as a dip or sauce.

## Insider Tips

- Use lime juice instead of lemon for a tangier flavor
- Add chopped fresh herbs like parsley or cilantro for freshness

**1 serving**

**15 minutes**

**Easy**

# Iraqi Tomato Sauce

## Ingredients:

- 1 cup plain yogurt
- 2 cloves garlic, minced
- 1 tablespoon lemon juice
- 1 tablespoon olive oil
- Salt and pepper to taste

A creamy and pungent garlic sauce that adds a burst of flavor to Lebanese cuisine. Legend has it that Toum was created by a Lebanese chef who wanted to elevate the humble garlic into a culinary masterpiece.

## Directions

1. In a bowl, combine yogurt, minced garlic, lemon juice, olive oil, salt, and pepper.
2. Whisk until well blended.
3. Adjust seasoning to taste.
4. Serve as a dipping sauce or drizzle over grilled meats or vegetables.

## Insider Tips

- Use Greek yogurt for a thicker sauce
- Add chopped fresh dill or mint for extra flavor

**1 serving**

**20 minutes**

# Iraqi Green Chutney

*mmmmmmmm*

## Ingredients:

- 2 cups chopped tomatoes
- 1/4 cup tomato paste
- 1/4 cup chopped onions
- 2 cloves garlic, minced
- 1 teaspoon dried oregano
- 1 teaspoon dried basil
- 1/2 teaspoon sugar
- Salt and pepper to taste
- 2 tablespoons olive oil

**Easy**

A tangy and flavorful sauce made from ripe tomatoes and aromatic spices, perfect for pasta, pizzas, or as a dipping sauce. Iraqi tomato sauce is a versatile condiment that adds a touch of Mediterranean flair to any dish.

## Directions

1. In a saucepan, heat olive oil over medium heat.
2. Sauté onions and garlic until translucent.
3. Add chopped tomatoes, tomato paste, oregano, basil, sugar, salt, and pepper.
4. Simmer for 15-20 minutes, stirring occasionally, until the sauce thickens.
5. Adjust seasoning to taste.

## Insider Tips

- Use fresh herbs like thyme or rosemary for added aroma
- Add a pinch of red pepper flakes for a spicy kick

Easy

# Iraqi Date Syrup (Dibs)

## Ingredients:

- 1 cup fresh cilantro leaves
- 1/2 cup fresh parsley leaves
- 1 green chili, chopped
- 2 cloves garlic, minced
- 2 tablespoons lemon juice
- 1/2 teaspoon ground cumin
- Salt to taste
- 2 tablespoons olive oil

A vibrant and zesty chutney made with fresh herbs, lemon juice, and spices, perfect for dipping or as a condiment. Iraqi green chutney adds a burst of flavor to grilled meats, sandwiches, or appetizers.

## Directions

1. In a food processor, combine cilantro, parsley, green chili, minced garlic, lemon juice, cumin, salt, and olive oil.
2. Blend until smooth, adding more oil if needed.
3. Adjust seasoning to taste.
4. Serve as a dip or spread.

## Insider Tips

- Add a handful of mint leaves for extra freshness
- Substitute green chili with jalapeño for a milder version

**1 serving**

**60 minutes**

# Iraqi Pomegranate Molasses

## Ingredients:

- 4 cups pomegranate juice
- 1/2 cup sugar
- 1 tbsp lemon juice
- Pinch of salt

**Normal**

Iraqi Pomegranate Molasses, a tangy-sweet syrup, has its roots in the ancient Mesopotamian region, now Iraq. It's made by reducing pomegranate juice, creating a versatile ingredient for both sweet and savory dishes.

## Directions

1. In a saucepan, combine pomegranate juice, sugar, lemon juice, and salt.
2. Bring to a boil, then reduce heat and simmer for about 50-60 minutes, stirring occasionally, until thickened.
3. Let it cool, then transfer to a bottle.
4. Store in the refrigerator for up to 1 month.
5. Use in dressings, marinades, desserts, and cocktails.

## Insider Tips

- Cranberry juice can be used as a substitute for pomegranate juice.
- Honey or maple syrup can replace sugar.

**1 serving**

**45 minutes**

**Easy**

# Iraqi Mango Chutney

## Ingredients:

- 2 ripe mangoes, diced
- 1 onion, finely chopped
- 1/2 cup vinegar
- 1/2 cup sugar
- 1/2 tsp salt
- 1/4 tsp ground cloves
- 1/4 tsp ground cinnamon
- 1/4 tsp ground ginger
- 1/4 tsp ground cumin
- Pinch of cayenne pepper (optional)

Iraqi Mango Chutney is a delightful condiment with a blend of sweet and tangy flavors. Originating from Iraq's rich culinary heritage, it's a perfect accompaniment to grilled meats, sandwiches, or cheese platters.

## Directions

1. In a saucepan, combine all ingredients and bring to a boil.
2. Reduce heat and simmer for 30-40 minutes, stirring occasionally, until thickened.
3. Let it cool, then transfer to jars.
4. Store in the refrigerator for up to 2 weeks.
5. Serve with your favorite dishes.

## Insider Tips

- Pineapple or papaya can be used instead of mango for variation.
- Apple cider vinegar can replace regular vinegar.

1 serving

15 minutes

Easy

# Iraqi Walnut Sauce

## Ingredients:

- 1 cup walnuts, toasted
- 1/2 cup plain yogurt
- 1 clove garlic, minced
- 1 tbsp olive oil
- 1 tbsp lemon juice
- Salt and pepper to taste
- Chopped parsley for garnish

Iraqi Walnut Sauce, also known as 'Dijaj bi Joz', is a creamy and nutty sauce from Iraq, traditionally served with chicken dishes. Its rich flavor and smooth texture make it a favorite in Iraqi cuisine.

## Directions

1. In a blender, combine toasted walnuts, yogurt, garlic, olive oil, lemon juice, salt, and pepper.
2. Blend until smooth and creamy.
3. Adjust seasoning to taste.
4. Transfer to a bowl, garnish with parsley.
5. Serve as a sauce for grilled or roasted chicken dishes.

## Insider Tips

- Almonds or cashews can be used instead of walnuts.
- Greek yogurt can replace plain yogurt for a thicker sauce.

# Iraqi Red Pepper Paste (Harissa)

**1 serving**

**30 minutes**

## Ingredients:

- 10 dried red chili peppers, seeded
- 3 cloves garlic
- 1 tsp cumin
- 1 tsp coriander
- 1/2 tsp caraway seeds
- 1/4 cup olive oil
- Salt to taste
- Lemon juice (optional)

Iraqi Red Pepper Paste, also known as Harissa, is a fiery and flavorful condiment used in Iraqi and Middle Eastern cuisines. Its origins date back centuries, adding heat and depth to dishes like stews, soups, and marinades.

## Directions

1. Soak dried chili peppers in hot water for 30 minutes, then drain.
2. In a food processor, blend peppers, garlic, spices, and olive oil until smooth.
3. Add salt and lemon juice if desired, adjust seasoning.
4. Transfer to a jar, cover with a thin layer of olive oil.
5. Store in the refrigerator and use as needed in various recipes.

## Insider Tips

- Paprika can be used instead of dried chili peppers for a milder flavor.
- Tomato paste can add richness and color if desired.

**Easy**

# Sumac Yogurt Sauce

## Ingredients:

- 1 cup plain yogurt
- 1-2 tbsp sumac
- 1 clove garlic, minced
- 1 tbsp olive oil
- Salt and pepper to taste
- Chopped mint for garnish

Sumac Yogurt Sauce is a tangy and creamy dressing commonly used in Iraqi and Middle Eastern cuisines. It's made with sumac, a tart spice, giving it a unique flavor profile that pairs well with grilled meats or salads.

## Directions

1. In a bowl, combine yogurt, sumac, minced garlic, olive oil, salt, and pepper.
2. Mix well until smooth and creamy.
3. Adjust seasoning to taste.
4. Garnish with chopped mint.
5. Serve as a dressing for salads, dips, or a sauce for grilled meats.

## Insider Tips

- Lemon juice can be added for extra tang.
- Dill or cilantro can replace mint for a different flavor.

# Chapter 9:
# Desserts - Pastries

1 serving

60 minutes

# Baklava

## Ingredients:

- 1 package phyllo dough
- 1 cup walnuts, chopped
- 1 cup almonds, chopped
- 1 cup butter, melted
- 1 cup sugar
- 1 cup water
- 1/2 cup honey
- 1 teaspoon cinnamon powder
- 1 teaspoon vanilla extract
- Optional: ground pistachios for garnish

## Insider Tips

- Use pecans or pistachios instead of walnuts and almonds.
- Substitute ghee for butter for a richer flavor.
- Add a pinch of nutmeg or cloves to the nut mixture for a warm spice flavor.
- Use agave syrup or maple syrup instead of honey in the syrup.

**Normal**

Baklava, a delectable pastry, has a rich history dating back to the Ottoman Empire. Its layers of flaky phyllo dough, nuts, and sweet syrup make it a favorite dessert in many Middle Eastern and Mediterranean cuisines. Did you know? Baklava's precise origins are debated, with various cultures claiming its invention. However, one thing is certain —it's a beloved treat enjoyed worldwide.

## Directions

1. Preheat oven to 350°F (175°C) and grease a baking dish.
2. In a bowl, combine chopped walnuts, almonds, sugar, cinnamon powder, and vanilla extract.
3. Layer half of the phyllo sheets in the baking dish, brushing each layer with melted butter.
4. Spread the nut mixture evenly over the phyllo layers.
5. Layer the remaining phyllo sheets on top, again brushing each layer with melted butter.
6. Use a sharp knife to cut the Baklava into diamond or square shapes.
7. Bake in the preheated oven for 45-50 minutes or until golden brown and crispy.
8. While the Baklava bakes, make the syrup by boiling water, sugar, honey, and a splash of lemon juice until slightly thickened.
9. Once baked, pour the hot syrup over the hot Baklava, allowing it to soak in.
10. Garnish with ground pistachios if desired.
11. Allow the Baklava to cool completely before serving.

1 serving

40 minutes

# Basbousa (Semolina Cake)

## Ingredients:

- 1 cup semolina
- 1/2 cup desiccated coconut
- 1/2 cup sugar
- 1/2 cup plain yogurt
- 1/4 cup vegetable oil
- 1 teaspoon baking powder
- 1/2 cup blanched almonds or pine nuts for garnish
- For the syrup: 1 cup sugar, 1 cup water, 1 tablespoon lemon juice, 1 tablespoon rose water

## Insider Tips

- Use almond flour or coconut flour for a gluten-free version.
- Substitute Greek yogurt for plain yogurt for added richness.
- Replace vegetable oil with melted butter for a buttery flavor.
- Add a pinch of cardamom or cinnamon to the batter for a warm spice kick.

Basbousa, also known as Semolina Cake, is a delightful dessert popular in Middle Eastern and Mediterranean cuisines. Its moist texture and sweet syrup make it a favorite for tea or coffee gatherings. Fun fact: Basbousa is often served during celebrations and festivals, symbolizing happiness and good fortune.

## Directions

1. Preheat oven to 350°F (175°C) and grease a baking dish.
2. In a bowl, combine semolina, desiccated coconut, sugar, plain yogurt, vegetable oil, and baking powder until well mixed.
3. Pour the batter into the greased baking dish and smooth the top with a spatula.
4. Using a knife, score the surface of the batter into diamond or square shapes.
5. Place a blanched almond or pine nut in the center of each shape.
6. Bake in the preheated oven for 30-35 minutes or until golden brown and a toothpick inserted into the center comes out clean.
7. While the Basbousa bakes, prepare the syrup by boiling sugar, water, lemon juice, and rose water until slightly thickened.
8. Once baked, pour the hot syrup over the hot Basbousa, allowing it to soak in.
9. Let the Basbousa cool completely before cutting and serving.

Normal

# Iraqi Date Cookies (Kleicha)

## Ingredients:

2 cups all-purpose flour
1/2 cup butter, softened
1/4 cup sugar
1/4 cup warm milk
1 tsp yeast
1/2 tsp ground cardamom
1/2 tsp ground cinnamon
1/2 cup date paste
1/4 cup chopped nuts (optional)
Powdered sugar for dusting

Iraqi Date Cookies, also known as Kleicha, are traditional treats enjoyed during festive occasions in Iraq. They are filled with a sweet date paste and infused with aromatic spices, creating a delightful blend of flavors.

## Directions

1. In a bowl, mix flour, butter, sugar, warm milk, yeast, cardamom, and cinnamon to form a dough.
2. Roll out the dough and cut into circles.
3. Spoon date paste onto each circle, sprinkle with chopped nuts if using, and fold over to seal.
4. Press the edges with a fork to crimp.
5. Place cookies on a baking sheet and bake at 350°F (180°C) for 15-20 minutes or until golden.
6. Dust with powdered sugar before serving.

## Insider Tips

Use almond or coconut flour for a gluten-free option.

Normal

# Ma'amoul (Stuffed Date Cookies)

munumunummun

## Ingredients:

2 cups semolina flour
1/2 cup butter, melted
1/4 cup sugar
1/4 cup warm milk
1/2 tsp yeast
1/2 tsp ground mahlab (optional)
1/2 tsp ground cinnamon
1/2 cup date or nut paste
Powdered sugar for dusting

Ma'amoul is a beloved Middle Eastern dessert, particularly popular in Lebanon and Syria. These delicate cookies are filled with a sweet date or nut paste, creating a delightful treat for special occasions.

## Directions

1. Combine semolina flour, melted butter, sugar, warm milk, yeast, mahlab, and cinnamon to form a dough.
2. Divide dough into balls and flatten each ball into a disc.
3. Place a spoonful of date or nut paste in the center of each disc.
4. Fold the edges over to seal and shape into a cookie.
5. Place cookies on a baking sheet and bake at 350°F (180°C) for 20-25 minutes or until golden.
6. Dust with powdered sugar before serving.

## Insider Tips

Use pistachios or walnuts for the filling.

# Kunafa

## Ingredients:

1 lb shredded phyllo dough
1 cup butter, melted
1 lb mozzarella cheese, shredded
1/2 cup ricotta cheese
1/2 cup sugar syrup
Crushed pistachios for garnish
Rosewater (optional)

## Insider Tips

Use kataifi dough as a substitute for shredded phyllo.

1 serving

45 minutes

Kunafa, also known as Knafeh, is a popular Middle Eastern dessert made with shredded phyllo dough, cheese, and sweet syrup. Its origins trace back to the Ottoman Empire and it's cherished for its crispy texture and gooey filling.

## Directions

1. Mix shredded phyllo dough with melted butter until coated.
2. Press half of the mixture into a greased baking dish to form a crust.
3. Combine mozzarella and ricotta cheese, then spread over the crust.
4. Cover with the remaining phyllo dough mixture.
5. Bake at 350°F (180°C) for 30-35 minutes or until golden brown.
6. Remove from oven and pour sugar syrup evenly over the hot kunafa.
7. Sprinkle with crushed pistachios and a few drops of rosewater if desired.
8. Serve warm and enjoy the gooey goodness!

# Qatayef (Stuffed Pancakes)

## Ingredients:

2 cups all-purpose flour
1 tsp instant yeast
1 tbsp sugar
1/2 tsp baking powder
1 1/2 cups warm water
1 cup sweet cheese or nut filling
Oil for frying
Powdered sugar for dusting

## Insider Tips

Use cream cheese or walnuts for the filling.

**Easy**

Qatayef are sweet stuffed pancakes popular in the Levant region, especially during Ramadan. They are filled with a variety of fillings like sweet cheese, nuts, or dates, then folded and fried to golden perfection.

## Directions

1. Mix flour, yeast, sugar, and baking powder in a bowl.
2. Gradually add warm water to form a smooth batter.
3. Let the batter rest for 10 minutes.
4. Heat a non-stick pan and pour a small amount of batter to make a pancake.
5. Cook until bubbles form on the surface, then flip and cook the other side.
6. Place a spoonful of sweet cheese or nut filling on one half of the pancake.
7. Fold the pancake in half to cover the filling, then seal the edges.
8. Fry the stuffed pancakes in oil until golden brown on both sides.
9. Drain excess oil and dust with powdered sugar before serving.

4 servings

60 minutes

# Rice Pudding (Roz Bel Laban)

## Ingredients:

- 1/2 cup white rice
- 4 cups whole milk
- 1/2 cup sugar
- 1 teaspoon vanilla extract
- Ground cinnamon for garnish

Embark on a journey to culinary bliss with Rice Pudding, a timeless dessert cherished for its creamy texture and delicate sweetness. A delightful treat for any occasion!

## Directions

1. Rinse the rice under cold water until the water runs clear. Drain.
2. In a saucepan, combine rice, milk, and sugar. Bring to a boil, then reduce heat and simmer for 45-50 minutes, stirring occasionally.

## Insider Tips

- Use brown rice for a nuttier flavor.<br>- Substitute almond or coconut milk for a dairy-free option.<br>- Add raisins or chopped nuts for extra texture.

**1 serving**

**120 minutes**

**Easy**

# Iraqi Cinnamon Rolls

## Ingredients:

1 cup all-purpose flour
1/4 cup warm milk
2 tbsp sugar
2 tbsp melted butter
1/2 tsp salt
1 tsp active dry yeast

Discover the ancient sweetness of Iraqi cuisine with these delectable cinnamon rolls. Originating from Iraqi homes, these rolls have a rich history of delighting families.

## Directions

1. In a bowl, mix warm milk, sugar, and yeast. Let it sit for 5 minutes.
2. Add flour, salt, and melted butter. Knead until smooth.
3. Roll out the dough, sprinkle with cinnamon sugar, and roll it up.
4. Cut into rolls and bake at 350°F for 20 minutes.
5. Glaze with icing.

## Insider Tips

All-purpose flour can be substituted with gluten-free flour.

**Normal**

1 serving

60 minutes

# Iraqi Sweet Dumplings

## Ingredients:

1 cup semolina
1/4 cup sugar
1/4 cup melted butter
1 tsp baking powder
1/2 cup milk
1/4 cup water
1/4 cup honey

Dive into the sweetness of Iraqi culture with these delightful dumplings. A cherished treat, loved for generations.

## Directions

1. Mix semolina, sugar, baking powder, and melted butter.
2. Add milk and water to form a dough.
3. Shape into dumplings and fry until golden.
4. Drizzle with honey.

## Insider Tips

Use almond milk for a dairy-free option.

Iraqi Sweet Dumplings (Zalabia),100

# Iraqi Date Rolls

## Ingredients:

1 cup dates, pitted
1 cup walnuts
1/4 cup shredded coconut
1 tsp vanilla extract
1/2 tsp cinnamon
Pinch of salt

**1 serving**

**90 minutes**

**Easy**

Embark on a journey of flavors with these Iraqi Date Rolls. A timeless delicacy that captivates with every bite.

## Directions

1. Blend dates, walnuts, coconut, vanilla, cinnamon, and salt until a sticky mixture forms.
2. Roll into logs.
3. Chill in the fridge.
4. Slice and serve.

## Insider Tips

Almonds can be used instead of walnuts.

# Chapter 10: Desserts - Puddings and Custards

**1 serving**

**10 minutes**

**Easy**

# Mahalabia (Milk Pudding)

## Ingredients:

1/4 cup cornstarch
2 cups milk (whole or low-fat)
1/4 cup sugar
1 teaspoon rose water or vanilla extract
Ground pistachios or almonds for garnish

Mahalabia, a luscious Milk Pudding, traces its origins to the Middle East and has captured hearts worldwide with its silky texture and delicate flavor. This delightful dessert is a testament to simplicity at its finest, showcasing the magic that can be created with just a few basic ingredients.

## Directions

1. In a saucepan, whisk together cornstarch, milk, sugar, and rose water until smooth.
2. Cook over medium heat, stirring constantly, until the mixture thickens and coats the back of a spoon.
3. Pour the pudding into serving bowls or glasses and refrigerate until set, about 2 hours.
4. Garnish with ground pistachios or almonds before serving.

## Insider Tips

Use almond milk or coconut milk for a dairy-free version.

**1 serving**

**45 minutes**

# Iraqi Rice Pudding with Rosewater

## Ingredients:

1/4 cup rice, 1 cup milk
2 tbsp sugar
1/4 tsp rosewater
chopped pistachios and almonds for garnish

**Normal**

This timeless dessert from Iraq combines the creaminess of rice pudding with the fragrant essence of rosewater, a true culinary gem.

## Directions

1. Cook rice in milk until soft and creamy.
2. Add sugar and rosewater, stir until well combined.
3. Serve warm or chilled, garnished with chopped pistachios and almonds.

## Insider Tips

Use almond milk for a dairy-free option.

1 Serving

60 minutes

# Saffron and Cardamom Pudding

## Ingredients:

1/4 cup semolina
1 cup milk
2 tbsp sugar
a pinch of saffron threads
1/4 tsp ground cardamom
chopped nuts for garnish

Easy

Originating from the Middle East, this pudding captivates with the luxurious flavors of saffron and the aromatic touch of cardamom.

## Directions

1. In a saucepan, cook semolina in milk until thickened.
2. Add sugar, saffron, and cardamom, mix well.
3. Pour into serving dishes, garnish with chopped nuts.

## Insider Tips

Replace saffron with turmeric for a similar color.

**Normal**

1 Serving

50 minutes

# Umm Ali (Egyptian Bread Pudding)

## Ingredients:

2 sheets phyllo pastry
1 cup milk
2 tbsp sugar
1/4 cup mixed nuts (almonds, pistachios, walnuts)
2 tbsp raisins
a pinch of cinnamon and nutmeg

Umm Ali, a traditional Egyptian delight, features layers of phyllo pastry soaked in milk and crowned with nuts and raisins.

## Directions

1. Tear phyllo pastry into pieces and place in a baking dish.
2. Mix milk and sugar, pour over the pastry.
3. Top with nuts, raisins, cinnamon, and nutmeg.
4. Bake until golden and bubbly.
5. Serve warm.

## Insider Tips

Use puff pastry if phyllo pastry is unavailable.

**Easy**

1 Serving

40 minutes

# Iraqi Bread Pudding

## Ingredients:

2 cups stale bread cubes
1 cup milk
2 tbsp sugar
1/4 tsp cinnamon powder
chopped nuts for garnish
caramel sauce for drizzling

This Iraqi delicacy transforms leftover bread into a heavenly dessert, infused with flavors of cinnamon, nuts, and caramel sauce.

## Directions

1. Soak bread cubes in milk until softened.
2. Add sugar and cinnamon, mix well.
3. Transfer to a baking dish, sprinkle with nuts.
4. Bake until golden and crispy.
5. Drizzle with caramel sauce before serving.

## Insider Tips

Serve with whipped cream for added indulgence.

**1 serving**

**60 minutes**

Easy

# Iraqi Style Rice Custard

## Ingredients:

- 1/2 cup rice, washed
- 2 cups milk
- 1/4 cup sugar
- 1/4 tsp ground cardamom
- 1/4 tsp ground cinnamon
- 1/4 tsp vanilla extract
- Pinch of salt
- Chopped nuts and raisins for garnish
- Rose water (optional)

Dive into the creamy goodness of Iraqi Style Rice Custard, a velvety dessert infused with aromatic spices and a hint of sweetness.

## Directions

1. In a saucepan, combine rice and milk, bring to a boil.
2. Reduce heat, simmer until rice is cooked and mixture thickens, stirring often.
3. Add sugar, cardamom, cinnamon, vanilla extract, and salt.
4. Cook for another 5-10 minutes until creamy.
5. Remove from heat, stir in rose water if using.
6. Pour into serving bowls, garnish with chopped nuts and raisins.
7. Chill before serving.
8. Indulge in the delightful flavors of this creamy dessert.

## Insider Tips

- Use almond or coconut milk for a dairy-free option.

**Easy**

# Semolina Pudding (Harisa)

## Ingredients:

1/4 cup semolina
1 cup milk
2 tbsp sugar
1/4 tsp cardamom powder
nuts and dried fruits for garnish

Originating from the Middle East, Harisa is a creamy semolina pudding loved for its comforting flavors and rich texture.

## Directions

1. In a saucepan, heat milk until warm. Add semolina gradually, stirring continuously to avoid lumps.
2. Add sugar and cardamom, stir until thickened.
3. Serve hot, garnished with nuts and dried fruits.

## Insider Tips

Milk can be replaced with almond milk.

# Carrot Pudding (Khabeesa)

**Normal**

1 Serving

45 minutes

## Ingredients:

1 cup grated carrots
2 cups milk
3 tbsp sugar
1/4 tsp cinnamon powder
1/4 tsp cardamom powder
nuts for garnish

Khabeesa, a delightful Middle Eastern dessert, celebrates the sweetness of carrots with a touch of aromatic spices.

## Directions

1. In a pan, cook grated carrots in milk until soft.
2. Add sugar, cinnamon, and cardamom, simmer until thick.
3. Serve warm, garnished with nuts.

## Insider Tips

Use honey instead of sugar for a healthier option.

Easy

# Pumpkin Pudding (Zalabya)

## Ingredients:

1 cup pumpkin puree
1/2 cup milk
3 tbsp suga
1/4 tsp nutmeg powder
1/4 tsp cinnamon powder
whipped cream for topping

Zalabya, an enchanting pumpkin pudding, brings together the earthy sweetness of pumpkin with a hint of spice.

## Directions

1. Mix pumpkin puree, milk, sugar, nutmeg, and cinnamon in a saucepan.
2. Cook until thickened.
3. Serve chilled with a dollop of whipped cream.

## Insider Tips

Top with crushed nuts for added texture.

1 serving

30 minutes

# Date Custard

## Ingredients:

- 1 cup whole milk
- 1/4 cup heavy cream
- 2 tablespoons sugar
- 1/4 cup chopped dates
- 1/4 teaspoon vanilla extract
- 2 large egg yolks

Normal

Indulge in a creamy, dreamy custard kissed with the sweetness of dates, a dessert that whispers of comfort and nostalgia.

## Directions

1. Preheat your oven to 325°F. Prepare a baking dish and set aside.
2. In a saucepan, combine the milk, cream, and sugar. Heat over medium-low until warm.
3. Add the dates and vanilla extract, stirring until well combined.
4. In a separate bowl, whisk the egg yolks. Slowly pour the warm milk mixture into the yolks, whisking constantly.
5. Strain the custard mixture into the prepared baking dish.
6. Place the baking dish in a larger pan filled with hot water to create a water bath.
7. Bake for about 25-30 minutes or until the custard is set but still slightly jiggly in the center.
8. Remove from the oven and let it cool slightly before serving.
9. Enjoy the creamy decadence of date custard!

## Insider Tips

- Use half-and-half instead of whole milk and cream for a lighter version.
- Substitute maple syrup or honey for sugar
- Use chopped figs or prunes instead of dates for a variation.

# Chapter 11: Beverages

1 serving

10 minutes

Super Easy

# Iraqi Chai (Tea)

## Ingredients:

- 1 cup water
- 1 black tea bag
- 1-2 tsp sugar (adjust to taste)
- 1-2 tbsp evaporated milk or regular milk
- Optional: cardamom pods, cloves, or cinnamon stick for added flavor

Iraqi Chai, also known as Iraqi tea, is a comforting and aromatic beverage enjoyed throughout Iraq, often served with hospitality and warmth.

## Directions

1. Bring water to a boil in a pot.
2. Add the tea bag and any optional spices if desired.
3. Let steep for 3-5 minutes, depending on desired strength.
4. Remove the tea bag and spices.
5. Stir in sugar and milk.
6. Pour into a cup and enjoy the aromatic Iraqi Chai.

## Insider Tips

Use honey or another sweetener instead of sugar.

**1 serving**

**15 minutes**

**Easy**

# Iraqi Coffee (Qahwa)

## Ingredients:

- 1 cup water
- 1-2 tbsp finely ground Arabic coffee
- 1-2 tsp sugar (adjust to taste)
- 1-2 cardamom pods (crushed)
- Optional: saffron threads for added aroma and color

Iraqi Coffee, known as Qahwa, is a strong and flavorful coffee with hints of cardamom, often served in small cups with a touch of hospitality.

## Directions

1. Bring water to a boil in a pot.
2. Add Arabic coffee and crushed cardamom pods.
3. Let simmer for 5-10 minutes to infuse flavors.
4. Remove from heat and let coffee grounds settle.
5. Strain into a small cup.
6. Stir in sugar and add saffron threads if desired.
7. Serve hot and savor the rich flavors of Iraqi Coffee.

## Insider Tips

Use ground cinnamon or nutmeg instead of cardamom.

Super Easy

# Jallab

## Ingredients:

1/4 cup Jallab syrup
1 cup cold water
Crushed ice
Pine nuts and raisins for garnish

Indulge in the rich flavors of the Middle East with Jallab, a traditional drink loved for its sweetness and refreshing taste.

## Directions

1. Pour Jallab syrup and cold water into a glass.
2. Add crushed ice.
3. Stir well.
4. Garnish with pine nuts and raisins.

## Insider Tips

None

# Tamarind Juice (Tamar Hindi)

Transport your taste buds to tropical lands with Tamarind Juice, a tangy and thirst-quenching delight.

**1 serving**

**15 minutes**

## Ingredients:

2 tbsp tamarind paste
1 cup water
1-2 tbsp sugar
Crushed ice

## Directions

1. Dissolve tamarind paste in water.
2. Add sugar and stir until dissolved.
3. Serve over crushed ice.

## Insider Tips

Use tamarind concentrate if paste is not available.

**1 serving**

**5 minutes**

# Ayran (Yogurt Drink)

## Ingredients:

1 cup plain yogurt
1/2 cup cold water
Salt to taste

**Super Easy**

Cool off in style with Ayran, a refreshing yogurt drink that complements any meal perfectly.

## Directions

1. In a blender, combine yogurt, water, and salt.
2. Blend until smooth and frothy.
3. Serve chilled.

## Insider Tips

Add a pinch of mint for extra flavor.

1 serving

15 minutes

# Mint Lemonade (Limonana)

## Ingredients:

1/4 cup fresh lemon juice
2 tbsp sugar
1/4 cup fresh mint leaves
1 cup cold water
Crushed ice

Easy

Quench your thirst with Mint Lemonade, a zesty and invigorating drink that's bursting with citrusy goodness.

## Directions

1. In a pitcher, combine lemon juice, sugar, mint leaves, and cold water.
2. Stir until sugar dissolves.
3. Serve over crushed ice.

## Insider Tips

Use honey instead of sugar for a healthier option.

1 serving

10 minutes

# Rosewater Lemonade

## Ingredients:

1 cup water
1 tablespoon rosewater
2 tablespoons fresh lemon juice
1-2 tablespoons honey or sugar
Ice cubes
Fresh mint leaves for garnish

Super Easy

Discover the refreshing elegance of Rosewater Lemonade, a timeless favorite with a floral twist. Perfect for sunny afternoons or evening soirees.

## Directions

1. In a pitcher, combine water, rosewater, lemon juice, and honey/sugar. Stir until well mixed.
2. Add ice cubes and garnish with fresh mint leaves.

## Insider Tips

-

# Iraqi Date Milkshake

## Ingredients:

1 cup milk
3-4 pitted dates
1/2 teaspoon vanilla extract
Pinch of cinnamon
Ice cubes
Optional: whipped cream and chopped nuts for garnish

**Easy**

Embark on a journey to the Middle East with this creamy and indulgent Iraqi Date Milkshake. A perfect blend of sweetness and richness.

## Directions

1. In a blender, combine milk, dates, vanilla extract, and cinnamon. Blend until smooth.
2. Add ice cubes and blend again until creamy.
3. Serve with optional whipped cream and chopped nuts on top.

## Insider Tips

-

# Mint Tea with Honey

## Ingredients:

1 cup water
1-2 teaspoons loose-leaf green tea or 1 tea bag
Fresh mint leaves
1-2 teaspoons honey or sugar
Lemon slices for garnish

Transport yourself to a Moroccan oasis with this soothing Mint Tea with Honey. A delightful blend of freshness and sweetness.

## Directions

1. Boil water and pour it over green tea leaves or tea bag in a teapot. Let it steep for 3-5 minutes.
2. Add fresh mint leaves and honey/sugar.
3. Serve hot with lemon slices for garnish.

## Insider Tips

Green tea bags can be used instead of loose-leaf tea.

# We have a small favor to ask

As we approach the final pages of "The Iraqi Home Cook: Experience Iraqi Gastronomy - A Middle Eastern Cookbook with 100+ Recipes and Stunning Pictures," we're thrilled to extend a warm invitation to you.

Crafting this culinary masterpiece has been an enriching journey through the flavors and traditions of Iraq. Each recipe is a celebration of the rich culinary heritage of this beautiful country, meticulously curated to bring the essence of Iraqi cuisine into your kitchen.

Yet, even the most meticulously crafted dishes can benefit from feedback. If you encounter any flavors or techniques that don't quite meet your expectations, please accept our humble apologies. We are committed to continuous improvement and value your honest thoughts and suggestions.

Your review is invaluable to us as a small publisher. Your participation shapes the future of our culinary endeavors, guiding us in refining our recipes and sharing the delights of Iraqi cuisine with more readers.

As you explore "The Iraqi Home Cook," we invite you to savor not only the flavors but also the stories and traditions woven into each dish. And while you're here, why not discover more culinary treasures waiting to be unearthed under the Garden of Grapes?

Thank you for being a part of our culinary journey. Your support and feedback mean everything to us.

Warm regards,

www.ingramcontent.com/pod-product-compliance
Ingram Content Group UK Ltd.
Pitfield, Milton Keynes, MK11 3LW, UK
UKHW060820301025
8675UKWH00042B/639

9 798330 372010